Bill &
Shirley

Bill &
Shirley
a memoir

Keith Ovenden

MASSEY UNIVERSITY PRESS

For Alastair Bisley & Lydia Wevers
In friendship

The first word

I doubt if anything is really irrelevant.
Everything that happens is intrinsically
like the man it happens to.

Maurice Spandrell in Aldous Huxley's
Point Counter Point

Contents

Preface

This is a memoir of my parents-in-law, Bill Sutch and Shirley Smith.

I met my wife, Helen, their only child, when we were both graduate students at Oxford in 1967, and we were married in the Wellington registry office, suitably located in Anvil House, in late October 1971. There is no point in pretending that, as far as family relations were concerned, it didn't start badly. Shirley was deeply opposed to the marriage, and did everything she could to prevent it. Prohibition being impossible — Helen was nearly 26 years old — and persuasion ineffective, she implied some sort of rejection, thus launching a period of coarse adjustment to which we felt obliged to conform.

Despite the unprepossessing start, this is not a confessional text, but it is worth mentioning that I found all of this hard to understand. My credentials as suitor and husband didn't strike either Helen or me as all that bad. The support we received from Bill and Shirley's friends, as well as our own, suggested that they shared our point of view. But of course, as both Helen and I eventually came to see, as in all such matters of the heart and psyche, the situation — its effects and its consequences — were not really about us. They were about them.

Circumstances really do alter cases, and they do so under time's piercing arrow. I knew Bill only for the last four years of his life, but they were years of high incident and drama, both public and private, and ones in which his general orientation to the world suffered a savage reversal. In the spring of 1974, at the age of 67, he was charged with an offence under the Official Secrets Act which, were he to be found guilty, would surely condemn him to prison for the rest of his life. The case dominated the ever-excitable press, which was hardly surprising given the circumstances of his arrest, when he was apparently set to meet a Russian Embassy official on a city street on a dark night in heavy rain. Spielberg could hardly have set it up better. Speculation both before and after the trial, along with deeply hostile commentary from some quarters, threatened to destroy a reputation that had been built over a lifetime of prominence in and devotion to his home country.

By the time of his death in September 1975 he was a man badly in need of sympathetic loyalty. Nor did his life, as is generally the case with public figures trapped in controversies outside their control, cease after his death. Because Helen and I have had his presence in our own lives ever since, this memoir embraces elements that may look rather too much like biography: the subject is there, but he is long since dead. It is not my purpose, as others have felt so free to do, to root among his remains.

So I must say straight away that this makes no pretence of being a biography. It is, rather, an account of my own evolving understanding of the man, an understanding grounded not only in my direct experience of him in those last few years of his life, but also in the contents of his bookshelves, the items and objects in which he delighted, the memories of him that people occasionally confided to me, and the apparently endless streams of public and private commentary about him. Though frequently active in journalism and broadcasting in the 1970s, and again in the second half of the 1980s, I never contributed to any of the public commentary about Bill, but I have made it my business over the years to take the pulse of public response to his name and reputation.

What I have gained from this is reflected in what I have written. You surely do not have to reflect for long either on the course of Bill's treatment in the media, or on the enterprise of memoir writing, to see that it could hardly have been otherwise. I make no claims to biographical thoroughness. I have not read his voluminous papers, which are in the Alexander Turnbull Library. I have not read the many letters that he wrote either to his daughter or to his wife. I have not conducted interviews, systematic or otherwise, with the hundreds of people who knew him. This is a memoir, a special class of remembrance.

The position with Shirley is rather different. I knew her from a first meeting in 1970, when she visited Oxford, until her death at the end of 2007; rather longer even than she had known her husband, whom she had probably first met in 1941. Throughout those years our relationship evolved through more phases than the moon, driven first from hostility into familial intimacy by our children, her grandchildren, and then cemented into mutual respect through the life that Helen and I lived together, the books that I wrote (and she read), her gradually changing view of the world and eventually by her deep regret for much that she found troubling in her past. 'If only, if only . . .' she would say. Her final years were spoiled by slowly encroaching indications of dementia, then wrecked by a disabling stroke, but before this first stroke and its successors, she committed some aspects of this regret to paper in a series of autobiographical sketches about her childhood, her life at Oxford in the 1930s, her marriage to Bill, her struggles in the law. In a sense she wrote them for Helen and me, and she certainly wanted me to read them, but though I have relied on them a little here, I do not quote from them. Many of the sketches were written when she stayed with us in Poland one summer at the very end of the last century, under very special circumstances. We had become friends long since, but it was an unusual sort of friendship. I have painted it in colours that I hope capture its unique qualities.

The one confession I do make is that these memoirs have been committed to paper towards the end of my own life simply because I feel the need to clear my mind about them. Both Bill and Shirley were extraordinary people whom it was a privilege to have known. That our earliest encounters caused me significant pain is of small importance compared with the great profit that I derived from their encouragement and friendship. I had learned much earlier in my life that it is neither necessary nor desirable to be liked by everyone. Something that, quite possibly, Bill never learned. The virtue of patience, however, is that it can bring other and far greater rewards than the satisfaction it is so often said to provide in itself.

Some balance has to be sought in any memoir: a balance between the self and its private preoccupations at the time of writing, and the self in the world at some other, earlier times; between home and society as they were then as opposed to now; between intimates, acquaintances and strangers in an ever-shifting world of memory and deeds; between factual and reputational information about others that we have now as well as then. It can be a difficult experience to confront one's own past errors and ignorance, but the recompense of understanding far outweighs the costs, and may lead to real if limited enlightenment. It is in response to these reflections that I have appended to this memoir a short resumé of my views on biography, which I believe also attach to memoirs.

Helen has read this work with her customary dispassionate and loving attention. I would not have sought publication without her agreement, but the fact of its appearance in print does not signify her endorsement of either my memory or my interpretation. This is my memoir, not hers.

Keith Ovenden
Wellington
May 2020

The Lion &
the Weasel

A memoir of Bill Sutch

I

There were always going to be difficulties, though I was at first surprised by their number. Loyalty to his wife Shirley, who was deeply opposed to our marriage, meant, inevitably, that Bill sided with her, and felt unable to express what I came to detect as his anxiety about her inability to accept our relationship for what it was. It was immediately obvious that he was deeply attached to his daughter, and the danger of losing her over this controversy of the heart was clearly more real for him than it apparently was for Shirley. He gave us, as a wedding present, a set of Danish cutlery, though he addressed the gift only to Helen and satisfied his evident need — evident to me, at any rate — to apologise for the whole unnecessary imbroglio with the hesitant words, 'That will be all right, won't it?', as though the acceptability of our marriage imagined through a lifetime of eating together might find symbolic expression in his gift.

Then there was the matter of my profession, only then recently labelled, following American practice, political science. At Keele, my undergraduate university, where the subject had been presided over by Professor Sammy Finer, the subject was called political institutions. At Oxford, where

I had recently completed a doctorate, it was political studies. At Essex University, where I then taught, I was a lecturer in the Department of Government. I didn't much like the term political science myself, and had had some entertaining if fruitless conversations on the topic during my year as a master's student at the University of Michigan. It was in vain, however, that I pointed out to Bill (as I was encouraged to call him from the start) that the word science simply meant knowledge, and that we should leave it at that. For him, political science was anathema, qualifying those it identified as second-class intellectual citizens.[1]

This view seemed to extend to political philosophy on which, from time to time, I occasionally attempted discussion, or at least conversation. It seemed to be of no interest to him: a view that was later confirmed by the contents of his bookshelves when, after his death, they became more readily available to us.

Plato and Aristotle, Hobbes and Locke, Rousseau, Mill, Marx and Laski all belonged to Shirley, and dated from her years studying Literae Humaniores and philosophy (also called, with some slight derision, Mods and Greats) at St Hugh's College, Oxford. I never got the least hint that Bill had ever read any works by these thinkers. He was uninterested.

I came to the conclusion that it was practicalities which mattered, and that in these he had a tendency to autodidacticism. His background knowledge was confined largely to New Zealand and came not from the big ideas of philosophers, but from textbooks and manuals which, almost without exception, were empirical: C. A. Cotton's *Geomorphology of New Zealand*, Henry Suter's *Manual of the New Zealand Mollusca*, K. A. Wodzicki's *Introduced Mammals of New Zealand*, Ferdinand von Hochstetter's *Geology of New Zealand* (1864) in Charles Fleming's 1959 translation, and almost everything on plants and shrubs and trees.

When it came to knowledge, New Zealand was his obsession. And if he needed guidance he went to the top. For instance, we found a letter of early January 1945 from A. J. Healy, a botanist in the Department of Scientific and Industrial Research, in response to an enquiry from Bill, setting out the literature on New Zealand plants. Thomas Cheeseman, R. M. Laing and E. W. Blackwell, W. Martin on plants, H. B. Dobbie on New Zealand ferns, everything by Leonard Cockayne — Healy recommended them all. Bill clearly took the advice, because they turned up on his shelves. Healy's letter he dropped into a copy of the 1927 edition of Cockayne's *New Zealand Plants and Their Story* which Shirley, then aged 13, had received as a botany prize at Queen Margaret College in 1929. Family cross-fertilisation, the school prize endorsed by a DSIR specialist as a reliable source.

The evident fascination with the detailed character of his own country of which these volumes speak (I know of no other household with a copy of Thomas Broun's 1880 edition of *Manual of the New Zealand Coleoptera*), coupled with his immense retentive memory, could make Bill an indifferent companion. Helen has deep scar memories of summer holidays when she was six, seven and eight, of long hours on dusty roads under a hot sun while her father pronounced monologues on the geology, flora, distinctive bird life and history of each area through which Shirley drove them in their little old car. As children do, she blanked it all out. He was a born teacher, but she was the wrong age.

Helen told me how very different the situation was when, still a young girl, she went to the summertime Student Congresses at Curious Cove in the Marlborough Sounds and, later, the Workers' Educational Association Summer Schools at New Plymouth, where Bill was invited to give talks and lectures. There would be more than 150 people present, many in family groups, gathered for a camp-style holiday in which informal lectures and discussion groups about topics of current interest took place alongside home-made evening entertainments, charades, dances and community singing. These very happy occasions (I have seen the photographs) were a completely different environment for learning about New Zealand and the world. There Bill was a different sort of teacher.

Similarly with budding adolescent and young adult intellectuals. It sometimes seems as if a whole generation of male students and youthful public servants have recalled to me, over the years, their pleasure at being invited to labour on the site of the Ernst Plischke-designed house that Bill and Shirley were building on the hillside above Todman Street in the Wellington suburb of Brooklyn in the 1950s.[2] Hugh Price, later a distinguished publisher, remembered unloading and hauling gravel; Rod Alley, later a university lecturer, wielded a pick and shovel; Fergus McLean, later a New Zealand trade commissioner, along with other young recruits from the Department of Industries and Commerce, helped to mix concrete and haul building materials; while Shirley grubbed gorse and laid on the lunchtime sandwiches.

Some probably found the tasks a burdensome intrusion on their weekends, but all those I have spoken to have grateful memories of working beside this knowledgeable, greatly experienced man who was eager to impart what he had learned, and knew how to nurture and sustain their interest. Just as John Ruskin, in nineteenth-century Oxford, took his students roadbuilding with picks and shovels, so Bill secured a place of enduring affection among these young people as their contribution was rewarded with conversation, instruction and advice.

What I lost sight of when first I heard these tales was the reverse: the effect of these young people on Bill. I think now that he found in them exactly the kind of endorsement and recognition of his own value to the world that he very much needed. Their approval eased, without ever completely eradicating, his anxiety, uncertainty, hesitancy and deep insecurity. For some reason I didn't fit into their mould. I had had significant teachers of my own and did not need another, so that I failed to play back to him, through my grateful attention, his vital place in the world. And besides, my presence in his life really had little to do with him. I was there because of Helen, which must somehow have relegated him to a position of secondary importance — not something he was particularly used to. I was inattentive to the kinds of telling detail that would have led to greater understanding and toleration on my part.

There are always, in people's lives, apparently little things that may speak volumes about them if we can only notice and focus on them. I write later in this book about Shirley's pinks — small carnations that she nurtured. With Bill I later saw that I should have focused on his Buddhas. He collected perhaps as many as 20 small statues of the Buddha, generally in the lotus position and made for the most part of stone or inexpensive metals. Museum shop copies, they represent different strands of Buddhism: Indian, Sri Lankan, Cambodian and Chinese, and different eras. None is particularly valuable in itself. Why did he collect them? Bill had no Buddhist beliefs or tendencies himself. He was one of the least contemplative people I have ever known. His interest in the eminent anthropologist Franz Boas's theories of 'primitivism' in art may have stimulated an interest in keeping one or two examples of Buddhist veneration, but not 20 of them. Was he trying to tell us something? I have no answer, but surely they are suggestive.

One of Bill's Buddhas, this one made of bronze, 21.5 x
15 cm. Bill collected such things, but no one, least of all
Shirley, seemed to know why.

It was perhaps my misfortune to have encountered Bill too late in his day, for when I began to acquire some intimate knowledge of him, from the spring of 1971 to the winter of 1972 when I held a post-doctoral fellowship at Victoria University of Wellington, I was expected to spend many hours in his company. They were never happy. The ritual was dinner on a Sunday evening at Helen's parents' home, the spiritual breaking of bread at the altar of family. Present, too, would be Bill's sister — also called Shirley — who lived almost next door. She was a professional psychologist who had recently taken early retirement from the psychology service for schools. In the family she was commonly referred to as 'sister Shirley'.

Given Shirley and Bill's antagonism to our marriage, and the wound this had inflicted on Helen in discovering that her mother's love was not unconditional, it is hard even now for friends to understand why we saw this ritual endorsement of family as a necessary obligation. Surely we might have said, well, in the circumstances, perhaps we should stay away, or at least go less frequently. It is a testimony to the strength of Helen's personality, her determination not to let her parents drive her from the family, that we never adopted this option.

The circumstances, already unpropitious enough, were laced with an air of tension so intense that it hung heavy over the table like a Brent Wong geometric sky object, oppressive, angular, a form of mesmeric menace. The situation was not helped by Shirley's resistance to having outsiders, or even family, in her kitchen, so that any normal participation in the general minutiae of the dinner was denied me. No table clearing, no fetching and carrying, no washing-up. Helen's assistance, except in the preparation of food, was permitted, but even so there was an unstated threat of possible sudden reversal, of permission withdrawn.

Being left at the table with sister Shirley and Bill meant a desperate search for appropriate topics of conversation, in itself problematic — as the Marxists like to say. Here, the difficulty presented itself in the form of Bill's unworldly asceticism. His taste in food was solidly grounded in working-class experience and not a topic of interest. A dish of roast lamb, gravy and vegetables, enjoyable enough, hardly lent itself to culinary debate. Bill would not have read *Cuisine* magazine had it then existed, although I'm pretty sure he would have subscribed to it as evidence of New Zealand's increasing cultural and commercial maturity, and would have promoted it whenever and wherever appropriate.

Another conversational impediment was that Bill didn't drink, never had and never, to my knowledge, broke his teetotalism. Loquacity and the ease of social exchange that wine may generate, along with complex matters of terroir, vintage years, palate, grape varieties and so on, were denied us. Some said the reasons for his abstinence lay in his Methodist upbringing, that he had taken the pledge. Others, those with knowledge of his family background, that its sources lay in his mother's influence in getting him to acknowledge and reject his father's overindulgence. Part of it, as I came to see, may have lain in his parsimony.

Bill hated to spend money on what he thought of as irrelevant indulgencies. All this must have added up to a bit of a trial for Shirley, who loved a drink and gladly adopted my own views on the merits of wine, as well as her father's pleasure in good Scotch whisky, once the prohibitions of her spouse were removed by death and the path of our relationship had become less sticky. But again, this did not mean that Bill was against wine or other drinks per se. Entertaining diplomats, businessmen friends, colleagues from Industries and Commerce in the recent past, he served wine and other beverages, professed to being knowledgeable about them and urged their development in the New Zealand economy. He kept their products in his cellar and would occasionally speak with some knowledge about them.

But this, like so much else in his appetite for local knowledge, was book learning, not the transmission of experience and taste. Under his direction, Industries and Commerce published a handbook, *Wine in New Zealand*, in 1962, the same year that they sponsored a wine exhibition. When his contract as head of the department was not renewed in 1965, when he was still only 58 years old,[3] the then industry body Winemakers of New Zealand presented him with two antiquarian books — George Sutton's *The Culture of the Grape-Vine and the Orange in Australia and New Zealand*, published in 1843, and William Speechly's delightful 1790 *A Treatise on the Culture of the Vine*[4] — in gratitude for his many efforts on their behalf.

Simpler sources of conversation were also somehow prohibited. Bill had little time for television. One had been installed in the house only in the spring of 1968, after he had been hospitalised with a heart attack. He had a similar indifference to radio. It had never occurred to him to have one in the house, and Shirley had apparently found it a matter of disloyalty when she finally, rather courageously as I think she saw it, went out and bought one. Or rather two. Little Bakelite models that proclaimed their unimportance by their diminutive size. Shirley kept hers in the kitchen for the most part, where she could listen while cooking or washing up; Helen, as a schoolgirl, had kept hers by her bed: popular music, very quietly, after dark.

Indifference to broadcasting was coupled with the cinema and photography. I never heard of Bill going to see a film. And he certainly didn't own a camera, was never seen to take a photograph and showed little or no interest in it as an instrument of domestic record. But this didn't mean that he was against films or photography. He was a great supporter of Brian Brake, whose work he promoted and with whom he had some correspondence. And once he became chairman of the Queen Elizabeth II Arts Council (as it then was) he was quick to understand from Jim Booth and Ian Fraser, two of his young lieutenants, the need to support and develop an independent film industry here. New Zealand's presence in the world, its social, economic and cultural development, were what interested Bill, and anything or anyone of merit or substance that helped to develop them could expect to get his support.

I took a particular benefit from this through his promotion of the work of Kobi Bosshard, a young silversmith from Switzerland. Bill instantly recognised his work, spotted in the counter display case of the Hermitage hotel at Aoraki Mount Cook where Kobi was working as a mountain guide, as of significant originality and craftsmanship. He bought a piece for Shirley, asked to meet Kobi and then ensured that he was put in touch with speciality retail outlets. Through them Kobi found a market that enabled him to flourish and develop. Helen, who already knew of this connection, suggested we ask Kobi to make our wedding rings. A great and valued friendship has developed with him and his wife, Patricia, across the years. Bill's capacity to create linkages, personal, commercial, historical, was one of his strongest talents.

So it was that his appointment as arts council chairman by the Kirk government in 1972 seemed at once both rational and quixotic. An inspirational moment of lateral thinking on somebody's part. Had he any expertise in the field of visual and plastic arts? Bill's interest in art, as conventionally understood, seemed reserved for the modernist movement and not much else. Somewhere along the way he had befriended the American artist Alexander Calder, possibly in London in 1938 as Calder spent much of that year visiting from New York. It is equally likely that an acquaintance developed into friendship during the mid- to late 1940s, when Bill was at the United Nations and Sandy, as Bill knew him, was working in his farmhouse studio at Roxbury in Connecticut. Bill commissioned two very small pieces by Calder that were easily the finest items in his collection.

Allied to this was the role that he played in the creation of the Architectural Centre in Wellington in the 1950s. The historians of this endeavour, which was a common topic of reminiscence for both Bill and Shirley, so much had they enjoyed participating in it, describe Bill as '[b]y all accounts a charismatic man'. The centre was a focal point for every aspect of contemporary art, from town planning to pottery, sculpture, furniture design and the graphic arts.[5]

Beyond modernism Bill's interest was really in craft — which helps to explain his enthusiasm for Kobi Bosshard, who brought craft and modernism together — and in particular what was known then as primitive art: pottery, sculpture, weaving; cast bronze and iron Bhuddas from south and south-east Asia; ceramics, sculptures and utensils from Latin America and China's deep past. There was almost no background information about such things in the New Zealand of his youth, and his knowledge, as in so much else, was to be found on his bookshelves. And here the most important influence was surely Franz Boas through his wonderfully liberating book, *Primitive Art* — 'an attempt to determine the dynamic conditions under which art styles grow up'.[6]

Boas was professor of anthropology at Columbia

University from 1899 until his death in 1942, and I find it hard to imagine that Bill would not have availed himself of the opportunity to attend his lectures, or even introduce himself and get to know him personally, during his year of study there in 1931–32. It was Bill's knowledge of this book that informed his lifelong enthusiasm for primitive art, which in turn led him to champion Māori art and cultural artefacts and to collect works of both ancient and modern crafts.

Many, if not almost all, of the items that he accumulated were copies, which he bought from various museums around the world — including a particularly beautiful T'ang horse. There were, however, a few lovely exceptions in pottery and sculpture of works from China, Mexico and Cambodia which, though not expensive, show a true connoisseur's eye. His books on these subjects are an eclectic mix suggestive of the width of his interest, from Hugo Blattler's *Ceramics in Italy* and Ernst Rosenthal's *Pottery and Ceramics*, which includes, just as Bill would have wished, a deal of technical information about the processes of potting — kiln firing, slips and dyes; to Stuart Piggott's *Prehistoric India*, much thumbed; William Willetts' two-volume *Chinese Art*; and J. Alden Mason's *The Ancient Civilizations of Peru* — though this last was so stiff and unfoxed when I first opened it that its owner must never have had the time to read it.

Then there was his interest in design, which he shared with Shirley. Copies of Anthony Bertram's *Design*, Roger Fry's *Vision and Design* (a present from her father at Christmas 1940) and John Gloag's *The English Tradition in Design* all clearly belonged to Shirley. And I have no doubt that she read both of Nikolaus Pevsner's books, *An Outline of European Architecture* and *Pioneers of Modern Design*, just as avidly as Bill. But Bill took no particular *private* interest in the world of art. Galleries and exhibitions of works by the Impressionists, or European landscape artists, or Renaissance masters, or English portrait painters of the eighteenth century were not his sort of material.

Cast about as I might, there was little to cover the naked silences of the dinner table, where the less than lavish conversational fare was generally limited to the contents of books and periodicals and the current state of the garden. Books were always difficult because our interests at this time barely touched, let alone merged. I had recently finished writing a doctoral thesis on policy-making in British politics. My master's degree before that had been in the area of American politics and history. My post-doctoral research, on which I was then engaged, focused on European literature and politics in the 1930s. I felt in no need of guidance on the politics of the period — the general arrogance of youth I now recognise only too well — and my wide reading, from W. H. Auden to Yevgeny Zamyatin, lay way outside Bill's interest zone. I never saw him read a poem and we never had occasion to discuss a novel. Away from modernism and the primitive, Bill's interest seemed to be New Zealand. Full stop. Its history, geology, flora and fauna, peoples, economy, education system, crafts and skills, landscapes and communities, climate, trade, research and resources. On all of these topics he stood like a monument astride the sources, archives and literature.[7]

And chief among these was New Zealand history. He owned hundreds of books on this, his heartland topic, from Cook's *Voyages* to Ernst Dieffenbach's two-volume *Travels in New Zealand* of 1843; from William Fox's *The Six Colonies of New Zealand* (1851) to Richard Taylor's *The Past and Present of New Zealand; with its Prospects for the Future* (1868); and from Guy Scholefield's edition of *The Richmond–Atkinson Papers* (1960) to some 30

A Han horse and rider from Bill's collection, clay, 35 x 24 cm.
The rider is probably a musician, but has lost his instrument,
possibly a side drum.

or so volumes of the voyages of discovery published in facsimile by Cambridge University Press for the Hakluyt Society. Unlike some academic historians, Bill seemed to have no competitive animosity to other members of the profession. He admired the work of John Beaglehole and was enthusiastic in his recommendation of a new young generation of researchers. Tony Simpson's *The Sugarbag Years* was a Christmas present to us in 1974 and he urged me to read Keith Sinclair's ground-breaking *History of New Zealand*, in which the criticism of colonialism matched his own. He greatly admired *Moko* (1972) by Michael King and Marti Friedlander, and claimed to have been instrumental in ensuring that Michael received an arts council grant to work on his biography of *Te Puea* (1977).

It was in the garden at Brooklyn one late afternoon in the autumn of 1975 that I first met Michael, who was visiting to talk to Bill about his work. Another friendship I owe Bill. In similar vein he reported to me his interest in the career of Michael Bassett, with whom he had enjoyed some mild controversy over the latter's criticism of 'technical' faults in the 1966 edition of *Poverty and Progress*.[8] He would surely have enjoyed both Erik Olssen's biography of John A. Lee and Michael Bassett's account of the 1951 waterside dispute.

But these truths must be set beside another, less palatable perhaps. New Zealand history and all its adjacent fields were his subject, but if I ever wanted to discuss them with him, any of them, then I was destined for disappointment. What I had to do was listen. Bill did the talking. Monologue was the form, agreement the currency of exchange. It might seem, at this distance, a small price to pay, as he had much to impart, and an incredibly sound view of how history — both the sort that is written down and the sort that is not — not only shapes and binds us, but also betrays and exhausts us.

At the time, however, the price felt exorbitant. Bill's syntax had retreated from whatever storm waters of complexity it had previously navigated onto the shallow foreshore of the first person singular pronoun, so that it was more or less impossible to escape from the presence of his ego, the ever-present 'I' of opinion, fact, belief and interpretation. Neither Shirley, wife or sister, seemed equipped to interrupt. Helen, too, was a largely silent auditor. And I, fresh from a university in Britain at which discussion, argument and disputation were constants of daily life, was perplexed.[9]

As young people will, Helen and I interpreted these awkward occasions as something largely to do with us; that we were the problem; that if only I had not, like a worm in the apple, been present, the fruit of family pleasure would have been restored to ripe health. Eventually, the feelings of anxiety, not to say dread, became so great that we sought medical help, were prescribed valium (or possibly librium, I forget now) and duly turned up each Sunday evening thereafter mildly tranquillised against the tension of which we believed our union to be the principal cause.

I had plenty of time to reflect on the possible reasons for Bill's disfavour, imagining at first that it might be my nationality. I had been born and grew up in London, my accent was English and I carried all the baggage of the British class system. There was no obvious reason why Bill should like the English any more than I did, given his working-class origins. This belief of mine I discovered to be misplaced. He often asserted, surely correctly, that being brought up in New Zealand had allowed him to benefit from the possibilities opened by education in a way, and to a degree, that would never have been available in his parents' native Lancashire.

They were working-class people in an England where education was beyond their reach, opportunities for employment limited, personal growth and development just about impossible and the weight of class compulsion more or less irresistible, even for a skilled carpenter and joiner like his father. It was the first decade of the twentieth century, an age of domestic service, back-to-back slum housing, low industrial wages and job insecurity. His parents had been born into what looked and felt like a dead end.

Bill, who was only months old when his family migrated to New Zealand in 1908, grew up in a country that offered his parents work and hope, of which he in turn was the beneficiary. The sickly child grew to be robust, both sportsman and tramper. The ignorant child acquired an education, primary, secondary, tertiary. Briefly he became a schoolteacher before, at the age of 24, winning a scholarship to Columbia University in New York to study for a doctorate. The boy whose prospects would have been limited to industrial townscapes, polluted city air and all the ugliness of slum, slag heap and sewage pond, found a country of mountain and bush, beach and playing field. He was endlessly and, in conversation, boringly grateful for it.

It may be difficult now — though I saw it very clearly in the early 1970s — to understand what an immense transformation this was, how central to his whole self-image, and how deep-rooted it must have become in his appreciation of where his loyalties lay; the sort of bedrock understanding and sense of place that each of us carries through life. Even so, this deep affection for his homeland didn't entail a distaste for the British. Bill's quarrel with the world — and Britain certainly loomed large in this — was with colonialism, the exploitation, or theft as he saw it, of the resources of one people by another. And no memoir of mine is required to emphasise its importance to him: there is an entire book of his views on the subject.[10]

Rather more tangible evidence of Bill's opinion of the British, outside the inheritance of colonialism, lay in the periodicals that came into the house and which I was able to read of a Sunday evening in the half-hour or so after he came in from working in his garden and went to take a shower, before the weekly resumption of dinner table hostilities. There were the *Economist*, the *New Statesman* and the two *Listeners* — the one New Zealand (a rather different publication then from the health, culinary and financial advice magazine it was to become), the other British, both deeply serious in content. These were augmented by two publications from the east coast of the United States, the *Monthly Review*, an entertaining socialist publication, and the *New Yorker*, by turns, then as now, witty, serious, irreverent, intelligent, well written and thoughtful. These were his staple weekly diet of news and information about the world, and the world on which they reported in those days consisted more or less entirely of the industrialised countries of the Western alliance.

Reading these periodicals, I thought, surely provided the main source of his understanding of policy processes beyond New Zealand. A great deal of his professional activity at Industries and Commerce in the 14 years he served there as a senior public servant (all of them before I knew him) might be attributed to his opposition to colonialism, his training as an institutional economist and his understanding of the opportunities that existed in politics for innovation — what R. A. Butler called 'the art of the possible'. Much of the rest came from his weekly diet of these foreign periodicals.

Seen in this light, Bill's remarkable contribution to our thinking about economic development, while certainly prescient, had some quite conventional sources. The creation of the 1960 Industrial Development Conference and the 1963 Export Development Conference, and thorough planning to focus on export-led growth through industrialisation for import substitution, and value-added product development in the primary sector, were in the footsteps of British chancellor of the exchequer Selwyn Lloyd, and not those of Stalin, as much of the farming sector, and at least one later prime minister, considered.[11]

As with other aspects of his life, the evidence survived on his bookshelves. Between 1957 and 1965 Industries and Commerce published some 50 substantial reports on different aspects of New Zealand, ranging from regional surveys to specific industries — oil, steel, timber, television, farming; particular sectors — Māori, women; and activities — education, technical training, craft and design. Much of the background research for these would no doubt have been carried out by officials in his department, but his leadership was clearly the starting point, his intellect the guiding spirit and his writing the fundamental element of the finished products, all of which Bill presented to minister and Parliament.

The labour, given his many other responsibilities as a head of department, was enormous.[12] Both the physical stamina and the intellectual grip in this work were prodigious. And all of it, without exception, was directed at improving the lot of his fellow New Zealanders, extending their control over their own economic circumstances and their own society and its development. The publications, their purpose and direction, came as a torrent, leaving his opponents in the policy arena feeling, I now think, much as Labour supporters felt, 25 years later, under the deluge of Roger Douglas' entirely new policy settings of the mid- to late 1980s: flat-footed, dumbfounded, outmanoeuvred and intellectually drained.[13]

Bill certainly saw an enemy out there in the world at large, but the one I eventually detected was not Britain, or America or any other bogey of the political left, but those of his fellow New Zealanders who still called England 'home' and sought to perpetuate what he thought of as colonial arrangements. If you could name a single person emblematic of his intellectual distaste it would be Frank Milner, 'The Man', the 'eloquent protagonist of the Imperial idea' — fellow of the Royal Empire Society, rector of Waitaki Boys' High School, Ōamaru, for nearly 40 years and a tireless propagandist for the imperial ideal.[14]

This was rather heady stuff: a danger to intellectuals, especially when young, as I was when I first encountered it. Helen had tried to prepare me before we arrived in Wellington but I had to learn it for myself. Bill was a figure. He was talked about. There was gossip and argument. He rubbed some people up the wrong way, could be abrasive and intolerant. He seduced others with his power of argument, its forecasts and insights, his charm. He seemed to overwhelm just about everybody with the speed of his output. Bill was a great puzzle. People were in awe of him. Some of these same people may have detested him too, but would never say so publicly.[15] Somehow he had become a sort of law unto himself. Being related to him by marriage meant that others were inquisitive. It was hard to disguise my lack of enthusiasm, especially as it also became clear that Bill could be kind and collegial, generous in praise, thoughtful in criticism, affectionate in his attentions.

Thirty some years after his death, Helen and I went to

talk to the woman who had been his secretary when he was the head of Industries and Commerce. She made it quite clear that there had never been a boss like him, that she had never known anyone so considerate or thoughtful of her welfare. He was extremely demanding, especially with his output of letters, memoranda and manuscripts for publication by the department, but she loved working for him. No one could have wished for a better job. After his departure she refused to work for his successor, preferring to return to the typing pool and the much lower salary from which, nearly six years before, she had come. Her view, and her dismay at his departure, seems to have been shared by the entire department.[16]

As 1971 turned into 1972, and the relatives went off for holidays in different directions, our married life was temporarily freed from the constraints of family awkwardness and settled into great happiness, the oddness of dissension up there, as I thought of the house in Brooklyn, falling into better perspective. I was helped by Helen's lovely aunt Helen, a source of domestic calm and family advice, by the great educationalist Jack Shallcrass, who seemed to know Bill as well, if not better than anyone, by our friends Nigel Priestley and Jule Einhorn, with whom we spent many happy hours, and by Frank Romanowsky and Jackie McKenzie, who in the New Year of 1972 carried us off to a remote bach on Snake Point in the Marlborough Sounds, where we lived off the fresh fish and mussels that we took from the sea and talked into the night after, so it seemed, endless days of summer sun.

What was it, I kept wondering, that my father-in-law wanted from me? The frequency of that word 'security' in his writing seemed one possible guide. I read his *The Quest for Security in New Zealand*, which was published in 1942, not as a history book so much as a personal guide to its author, in much the same way that a biography may tell us a great deal, if not more, about its writer than about its subject. The English historian Tony Judt, 40 years later, captured some of what I thought in his conversations with Timothy Snyder:

> *That generation, born around 1905, was without question the most influential intellectual cohort of the twentieth century. They reached maturity just as Hitler was coming to power and were drawn willy-nilly into the historical vortex, confronting all the tragic choices of the age with little option but to take sides or have their sides chosen for them. After the war, young enough in most cases to avoid the discredit that fell upon their seniors, they exercised precocious intellectual . . . influence, dominating . . . the scene for decades to come.*[17]

There is a lot of truth in this as a general view of political motivation in the middle years of the twentieth century, but I think now that it applies not so much to Bill as to Shirley. Bill was always rather different, a man born of English Victorian parents into an Edwardian colonial setting, who had by his own efforts leapfrogged Georgian formalism and restraint directly into the modernist break with the past. The distance travelled, emotionally and intellectually, would have strained anyone. Bill it left vulnerable to self-doubt, uncertainty and insecurity, which he disguised from himself, and others, by an immoderate self-confidence and braggadocio.

W hat else was the extraordinary Plischke modernist house on the hill but a bulwark against the possibility of loss, of being thrust back into the vulnerability of past poverty? By its sheer statement of difference, its break with the cottage and villa styles of New Zealand's colonial architectural heritage, it rejected Bill's past and sought to replace it with a new self-made authority that owed nothing to antecedents and spoke bravely, in its demonstration of modernism and fine craftsmanship, of a confidence he wanted to communicate to others. He seemed to need that confidence, the particular vision of secure prosperity and all the remarkable industrious effort of his lifetime's work, to be recognised and endorsed. He positively *needed* all of us, his wife and sister, his daughter, friends and visitors, editors and colleagues, politicians and broadcasters, everyone, down to and including his son-in-law, to award him recognition and approval.

The immoderate self-confidence wasn't exactly new, either. As a young man he had made headlines at Easter 1933 when the small tramping party of which he was a member became trapped by such heavy rain, snow and high winds that the Tararua tracks on which they had set out became virtually impassible and the streams and rivers unfordable. The four of them, one with a badly damaged ankle, included his soon to be first wife, Morva Williams, whom I never met, and of whom I know almost nothing, though she lived to be a great age and always retained the surname of Sutch. They were more than two weeks gone, 11 days overdue. Search parties were organised, their lives feared for.

Then, quite suddenly, they were encountered by a search party from the Carterton Tramping Club walking down a path out of the bush, having successfully, after a long struggle, found a safe route down from the tops. Welcomed as the lost who had at last been found, Bill did not endear himself to everyone by observing that they were never lost, and had not been found. They always knew where they were, had followed good tramping practice for the conditions they had encountered and had successfully found their own way out.[18] Some tramping experts wrote approvingly of the ways in which the party had coped and survived, but affronted opinion and adverse controversy abounded in the newspapers.

A different sort of tramping story came up at the table, though I can't now remember the first time that I heard it. Perhaps it was something that Helen had told me about her father when we were first getting to know each other. After completing his doctorate at Columbia University in New York at the end of May 1932, Bill had gone to Europe and travelled on the continent. With the remnants of his student grant, he had gone mainly on foot, with occasional train trips and hitched rides. Finally there had been an epic walk that had started inside the Arctic Circle, and eventually taken him, via Soviet Russia, to the Caucasus, Afghanistan and into India, whence he had managed to get a cheap air ticket home.

It was an heroic journey and its telling was frequent enough to be widely known. He had certainly recounted it to Shirley — in September 1942 he gave her a copy of *The Quest for Security in New Zealand*, where he included it as part of the blurb about the author[19] — and she had admired it greatly at the time. It endorsed his reputation as a tramper of stamina and attracted astonished admiration. And it was, of course, hokum. By my twenties I had done a fair bit of long-distance walking of my own, knew well the limits of daily endurance of even the best hikers and could calculate easily the time required for a walk of this kind.

Of more interest here, though, is the fact that the letters Bill had written to his mother throughout the few months he was away showed — stamps still on the envelopes, details of daily experiences — that the walk was heavily fictional.[20] Why would he engage in this invention and persist in it over decades? I think it must have been that desire, or even need, for approval. And what was lacking in him that made him like this? Why should a man of such obvious ability and almost startling originality need approbation from the rest of us? And why go to such myth-making lengths to acquire it?

One part of the answer lay in the presence of a wilful streak in his character. Shirley interpreted this as evidence of Bill's categorical independence. He did what he wanted and was never going to be restrained by others. When the book he was invited to write as part of the national centenary celebrations in 1940 was rejected by its commissioning committee as inappropriate and unacceptable, he declined to make changes. He was paid for his work anyway, and given permission to publish elsewhere, which he did, though he must also have talked inside the family of having done so against the committee's explicit wishes, because this is what was passed down to me as the truth. The book came out in 1941 under the Modern Books imprint of the Wellington Co-operative Book Society as *Poverty and Progress in New Zealand*. It was said to have sold well. This was followed, in 1942, by *The Quest for Security in New Zealand*, which sold many thousands of copies worldwide as a Penguin Special and must have provided him with some financial independence.

This was hardly new behaviour. In the 1930s, when he was adviser to Walter Nash, the Minister of Finance, Bill wrote under various pseudonyms for the radical weekly paper *Tomorrow*. There was rumour later that he had been its Wellington editor, but there is no evidence of his editorial input. A Wellington contact at a time of much slower communication might be a better description. In the 1950s and 1960s he went on with this kind of writing, in different contexts, while he was working for Industries and Commerce. This was hardly the conduct of a good and faithful public servant.

He was breaking the rules, but he wanted us to agree that it was permissible because what he was doing and saying was right and ought not to be prohibited by the rules. Rules weren't just for others necessarily, but they were there to be broken. I doubt that he ever distinguished much between the social rules of conventional behaviour and the rather stricter rules of legal requirement. Within his strong moral code, no doubt bequeathed by his Methodist upbringing, an important element was his right to think and to live as a free man, saying whatever he wanted. You can get collisions out of this sort of thing.

I sensed rather than understood all of this. It only really clarified later, when Shirley felt able to talk to me more intimately, but at the time his obvious quest for an approval that I withheld was not going to endear me to him. I was more than happy to offer him allegiance as my father-in-law, but he couldn't — any more than anyone else — hope for my intellectual obedience. Perhaps this was, at the beginning, the nub of the problem with Shirley as well as Bill.

There is now much to regret in all this. Some of it was misunderstanding. But it was misunderstanding of an historical kind, not the sort for which Helen and I could possibly be blamed. Ignorance, always regrettable, cannot always be rectified, at least not in time to be of any use. The reason for my unacceptability, with which I satisfied others for many years, was supplied to me by Jack Shallcrass, ever eager to educate, who said that Bill and Shirley were opposed to my marrying their daughter 'because you are not Jesus Christ', suggesting a cause of rejection beyond rectification. In the end this was never really the case.

Left out of the mix — not exactly a ghost at the table, more a presence of what seemed to me brooding, even threatening, anxiety — is sister Shirley. She was 11 years

Two of Bill's most significant early books, published in 1941
and 1942. He had a sound view of how history not only
shapes and binds us, but also betrays and exhausts us.

younger than Bill, in many ways his favourite sibling, who he had greatly encouraged and supported through school, teachers' training college and university. She had accompanied Bill, Shirley and their baby, Helen, to London in 1946 and stayed with them there and subsequently in the United States. She and Bill had taken the lion's share of looking after their mother as she aged rapidly in the 1950s, and when Shirley's work eventually brought her back to Wellington after years in Christchurch and Dunedin, she had come to live in Brooklyn, more or less next door to her brother and sister-in-law in a house that Bill helped her to buy.

She had never married, and against severe odds successfully pursued a career in psychology, playing a major part in the creation of the psychological counselling service for schools. She shared with Bill a deep interest in gardening, which did supply them with one safe dinner table topic, from which, at that stage, I was content to be excluded. As usual, however, it consisted mainly of Bill telling Shirley what she should do.

But quite apart from gardening, it was clear to Helen and me that something else was going deeply wrong in their relationship. Much of the tension, almost physical in form, so dense did it become, seemed to be generated between and among them, with wife Shirley as some sort of marginalised observer, a witness to the disarray. As with everything else, Helen and I saw ourselves as the problem. This was because sister Shirley, without being too explicit about it, had welcomed me as Helen's husband to be. Unlike Bill and Shirley, she came to our wedding reception, as did her other brother and sister-in-law, Ted and Judy, and sought through demeanour and gesture to offer Helen a lifeline for the preservation of some sort of relationship with her parents.

This, obvious enough to Bill and Shirley was, we

thought, the reason for his displeasure with her. We believed that, like us, she came each Sunday to the dinner table because she was not going to allow proper relations to be dictated by unspecified and ill-informed judgements that risked rending the entire fabric of the family. Much later, after her death at the turn of the century, we were to discover that this was far from the whole truth.

Sister Shirley suffered dreadfully from Bill's arrest, trial and death. Like others in the family, she was subjected to vicious anonymous letters and phone calls, and innuendo in the street, and consequently shrank from social engagement. She retreated into the worlds of her close friendships and of her affection for her two grand-nephews, our sons. Often lonely, increasingly isolated as her friends died, she drank rather immoderately, which must, eventually, have undermined her health. Even so, she lived into her early eighties and, once diagnosed with breast cancer, chose her own death by resolutely refusing food.

As she aged, adrift on a sea of melancholy mixed with bitterness, and occasionally anger about the past, she had not really looked after either herself or her possessions, chief among which were her papers, both professional and private. Stored unsorted in some 30 or 40 cardboard boxes, they were put into store when her house was cleared, and it was not until 2007 that I was able to go through them and prepare those of any public interest to go to the Alexander Turnbull Library. They turned out to contain some surprises, many of them rather stimulating.

II

We have become accustomed in recent years to hearing life described as a journey. It can seem an odd kind of allusion, since none of us is free to choose its starting point. We do not select our parents and generally come to see our origins as a matter of chance. Equally, none of us knows where or how life is going to end. With a fortuitous start and no known destination, the journey, whatever our best efforts to give it shape and meaning, rather takes on the features of a magical mystery tour. Even so, the idea has acquired a grip on the public imagination, a favourite cliché in particular of celebrities and sportspeople when speaking of themselves and their careers.

The idea of the journey of life is not new, however. It has been around in one guise or another since *The Odyssey*, though in Ulysses' case the denouement was one of violent, murderous self-justification. Two broad attitudes towards life as travel and as metaphor for experience may be detected much later: in the title of volume five of Leonard Woolf's autobiography, *The Journey Not the Arrival Matters*; and in the words of the French writer Paul Nizan in his youthful book, *Aden Arabie*: 'There is only one kind of valid travel . . . And its natural end is the return. The whole value of the voyage lies in its last day."[1] Either what you do in the whole of your life, and not the events of its ending, is what is important and should be valued; or it is the way you finish your life that tells the truth of what preceded it, embellishing, or diminishing, if not negating, its value. Where each of us stands on this dichotomy can be revelatory.

Bill's last year, the end of his journey, was a catastrophe. In the spring of 1974 he was arrested and charged with an offence under the Official Secrets Act, specifically, of holding clandestine meetings with a recently arrived member of the Russian Embassy called Dimitri Razgovorov, the presumption — and it was only ever that — being that he was passing secrets to him. He came to trial in the High Court in February of 1975. He was acquitted, but over the ensuing autumn and winter months he was the target, not to say victim, of a press campaign orchestrated by the weekly newspaper, *Truth*. I assumed that its purpose was to provoke him into suing for libel so that, in any subsequent court hearing, he might be subjected to the kind of hostile interrogation in the witness box that he had declined to endure at his trial.

Nothing has occurred since then to persuade me that this was not the case. Nor have I heard any evidence to contradict my belief that members of the Security Intelligence Service leaked malicious gossip about Bill to *Truth* journalists at the invitation of the paper's main proprietor — a Wellington lawyer called Jimmy Dunne — and with the connivance of their own director.[2]

It was widely believed that Bill's death at the end of September 1975 was hastened by the pressure of this public humiliation, which was made worse by news that he was in default of his income taxes — a dereliction that brought a heavy penalty fine to add to the high cost of his defence lawyer at the trial, and yet more wickedly bad publicity. For a man who had been one of the handful of outstanding public servants in New Zealand's history, an immensely successful advocate of and for the welfare of his country, widely known and admired as an historian and advocate for universal social security benefits and an indefatigable propagandist for the nation's development, the fall could not have been greater.

In essence, he had lost his place in society, or at any rate been reassigned to another altogether different and malign one. He did not improve his situation by giving public statements reiterating what his lawyer had written on his behalf to Attorney-General Martyn Finlay in mid-October 1974, that the Russian diplomat he had been meeting apparently wanted to know about New Zealand views of Israeli Zionism and possibly wished to defect. The defection idea seemed plausible to me. There is a photograph of Razgovorov being escorted onto a plane and out of the country by a couple of men who look like Russian 'heavies' from a schoolboy comic. But I don't now believe that anyone really thought much of Bill's supposed speculation. It was a terrible misjudgement.

In private, away from the glare of this awful publicity, Bill seemed on the surface to handle the mess he had helped to create quite well. 'The question now is how I might continue to contribute,' he said; the assertive ego of the first person singular pronoun, though still there, now softened by this less abrasive syntax. At a supper hosted by his younger brother Ted and his wife, Judy, at their home in Eastbourne, Bill apologised to the family for his foolish behaviour. It was a poignant moment as we sat drenched in late summer evening sun in their beautiful garden. Judy, forever in character, called it her garth, which always brought a smile to Bill's face.

Dominion newspaper poster of 29 September 1975.
The sub-editor seems to believe that Bill committed
suicide, but both that and the 'stormy' were no more
accurate than much of the press coverage of his afterlife.

Bill's foolishness, of course, was to have met with a member of the Russian Embassy, which was the nub of the charge against him: the Union of Soviet Socialist Republics was construed as an 'enemy', and such meetings were forbidden in the Official Secrets Act.[3] He had been naïve.

Helen and I both found it fairly easy to accept this judgement of his behaviour, partly out of relief that he had avoided the long prison sentence that he would certainly have been given had he been found guilty, but mainly because it was obvious that he was far from well. If the meetings were supposed to be secret, why had he put the arrangements in his diary, and why were the meetings held in odd public places, out on the street? This was not rational behaviour. Critics and adversaries have continued ever since to refer to the meetings as 'clandestine' but was this really the right word? He might as well have made the arrangements over the phone, and met Razgovorov in Parsons' Bookshop café on Lambton Quay.

And there were other signs of mental deterioration. The failure to report his taxable income correctly in recent years, how imprudent was that for anyone, let alone a senior figure constantly in the public eye?

And over the previous few years he had supposedly been at work on a biography of former prime minister Gordon Coates, a man for whom he had worked at the start of his career and for whom he professed a great admiration. Yet he was clearly blocked in this endeavour and had made no progress; unusual in a man famous for a single-minded dedication to the work in hand. In the 1980s I eventually got around to reading his last two books, *Takeover New Zealand* and *Women With a Cause*, published in 1972 and 1973

Women with a Cause, published in 1973. His late
works were serious and prescient, but was he
still present in them, heart and mind?

respectively. Neither is terribly well written. They have little if any of the panache of his earlier history books. They seem like the work of someone going through the paces because he felt strongly about both topics but was weary of the whole writing business. They have the feel of the river running dry, the volcano exhausting itself.

He also gave the impression of being somehow lost, not abstracted by thought, but empty of it, as if adrift. It made him harder to understand when he talked, as though he was not connected to the subject matter in hand. An evening in late August, early spring blossom already in full flower on the rhododendron 'Cornubia', which he had planted some 15 years before, he met me in the driveway as I got out of the car. 'You'll be all right, won't you? There?' he said. I had no idea what he was talking about, but said 'Yes, of course' anyway. But what *was* he talking about? Had I parked in the wrong place? I relegated these incidental mysteries to the trivia basket. Helen, pregnant with our first child, was just two weeks away from giving birth and the focus of our lives, struggling to free itself from theirs, meant that my mind was definitely elsewhere, too.

Nevertheless, Helen and I discussed his seeming mental deterioration with friends, and after his death the idea got about that Bill may have been suffering from ischemic attacks that had damaged his decision-making powers, and led to his uncharacteristic behaviour, but there was little evidence of this in the autopsy. If there was something going wrong in his brain the causes were psychiatric, not physiological.

Sunday evening dinners remained sombre in the months after the trial, but the tension now was of a different kind. In addition to the strange mental behaviour, he was clearly physically greatly reduced from the tough, resilient tramper and gardener, strong of frame and muscle, whom I had first met four years earlier. He had lost weight, looked strained, turned food aside.

Shirley reported to Helen that his appetite had diminished; he no longer wanted or enjoyed his favourite dishes that she prepared. He developed constant diarrhoea and Shirley took to giving him food that she had processed in a blender. He spent more time in bed. By mid-winter he was suffering from hives. Shirley told us that she urged him to see a doctor, but he refused, apparently preferring to soldier on. By early September he was so obviously unwell that he finally consented to take medical advice. In the middle of the month he was admitted to Wellington Hospital, subjected to a broad range of tests and after some delay, because its advanced state was puzzling to the specialist, diagnosed with terminal liver cancer.

The autopsy showed that he also had cancer of the bowel, which was perforated: it was probably this that had metastasised to the liver. He had been sick for three or four years. He died just two weeks after the diagnosis. It was a remarkable feat of endurance, to have carried himself as he did for all that time. He must have been at first in discomfort and then in serious pain for a very long period, one that probably coincided with my first meeting him, and which endured and intensified through the short season of his attempted meetings with Razgovorov, and his arrest and trial.

No wonder there had been tense occasions at the dinner table. The man was mortally sick and his mind was elsewhere. But where exactly?

Some sort of satisfactory answer emerged from sister Shirley's papers. Three elements among them were of particularly absorbing interest. One concerned her own quite independent discrimination at the hands of the American authorities when, in 1953, she was denied a visa to take up a scholarship awarded by the American Association of University Women to study for a doctorate in psychology at the University of Chicago. Apparently her membership of the Christchurch branch of the NZ–USSR Friendship Society proved a threat to the stability of American democracy.[4] The rejection not only changed her life, but arguably had a regrettable effect on the whole development of psychological services in New Zealand schools. It is tempting for me to regard this as one true outcome of the Cold War: the hostile belligerence of and to what was supposedly our own side.

The second matter, of greater interest to me, was the discovery that sister Shirley was lesbian. The evidence existed in dozens of letters from her young friends of teachers' training college and university days between 1938 and 1945. She appeared to have discovered her sexual orientation some time in the mid- to late 1930s. Her papers include many letters from a number of young women with whom she was clearly intimate, and which are touching, funny, exuberant as well as secretive and sometimes sad. She wrote poetry, spoke in the university debating society, studied history under Beaglehole and Freddie Wood, psychology under Professor W. H. Gould.

The correspondence illustrates both the dangers and difficulties young lesbians felt and also their courageous and sometimes happy indifference to public morality. A few of these loving relationships became enduring friendships, lasting into her old age. I wasn't able to sort these letters, but put into order and properly identified, they would clearly contribute to a portrait of many aspects of New Zealand society from the 1940s to the 1990s. The correspondents include Jeanne Edgar, who became the director of Risingholme Community Centre in Christchurch, and Kate Shallcrass, whom I had counted as a friend when she was Jack's first wife, but as a young woman was known affectionately as Cato — her maiden name.

These papers also flew in the face of the family narrative, maintained throughout her life, that sister Shirley was conventionally heterosexual in orientation, but had been unlucky in love, particularly regarding one young man with whom she had formed a close relationship during a brief spell at University College London in the mid-1940s. There had been no reason to disbelieve this story. Helen had always known of it. It had been recounted to me by Shirley. So my instant understanding, as I sat on the floor surrounded by these lovely letters, was that Bill's sister may have been shielded, throughout her life, from the disapproval, rejection and humiliation that were to be expected from a prudish society. That this should have been done during her young life was no surprise. Social condemnation was endemic, and not only among working-class families. But much had happened since the 1960s, including a more or less complete transformation towards social tolerance, if not approval. What was previously called deviant was no longer to be stigmatised.

Perhaps Bill, for all his progressive opinion, including his apparently advanced views on women's liberation by the end of his life, was not able to dislodge his working-class outlook on sexuality. We knew that as a young man he had held to fairly rigid ideas of the different social roles of men and women. It was widely understood that he had married Morva, his first wife, to quell the indignant condemnation of her having accompanied Bill and two other men, unchaperoned, on the ill-fated and much-publicised

1933 Tararua tramping excursion. I certainly doubt that his
mother, whose good opinion was deeply important to him,
would have been thrilled by this behaviour. Amid all his
writings on society, history and economy, I was unable to
remember a single mention of sexual orientation as being a
matter for even cursory discussion. Among those of English
working-class heritage, heterosexuality was one of the
necessary givens of life.

Then another bundle of letters came into my hand. These
were written from New York by a woman called Mary
Josephson. Her husband was a professor of philosophy
at Columbia University and at some point held a visiting
professorship at the University of Sussex in England. They
had a son. From the internal evidence of the letters, scraps
of references picked up elsewhere, never mentally filed
but never forgotten either, it became apparent that Mary
Josephson was the same person as Mary Redmer, a young
woman who had worked, on secondment from a federal
government department, for the United Nations Relief and
Rehabilitation Administration in Europe at the same time
as Bill in 1946. This was before his appointment to the UN
in New York. He had then known her again in the United
States, where she returned to work for a while in Washington.
They had clearly become lovers. From her side of the
correspondence — and we have none of his — it was the
seminal relationship of their emotional lives, pivotal in its
effects on all his subsequent years.

I have tried hard, since making this discovery, to
interpret, from behaviour, syntax and reference, the state
of Bill's mind and feelings about this situation. We knew
that he was torn about his professional future at the end

of his UN appointment in 1950: whether to stay on in New York, where he had been encouraged to apply for several different appointments in the UN administration, to look for a position in Europe or to return to New Zealand. Shirley was adamant for return and he eventually acquiesced. I think now that Shirley may have guessed the truth about Mary Redmer then, and had fought hard, with typical determination, to retain him. Shirley believed that her role in getting him to return to New Zealand was decisive, but she was perhaps rather too emphatic in her belief.

The whole question of what Bill was to do in 1950 is complex and deeply nuanced. There is correspondence with friends in New Zealand who urged him not to return, that there would be nothing for him here. I think his personal feelings about responsibility towards his daughter, loyalty to his wife — which he undoubtedly felt — and deep commitment to his homeland were at odds with other emotions. It is hard to think of Bill as a sentimental man, but in one letter to a friend written in 1946 he says how much he yearns for 'the mountains behind Nelson' and even 'the wind on the corner of Waterloo Quay'. There is enough evidence to suggest that this conflict in him, for all the physical and social attractions of his homeland versus the temptations of freedom and a bigger career in the outside world, never ceased.

It remains, of course, a common enough dichotomy among his compatriots to this day: whether to stay or to go, to come home or to commit abroad. The role of Mary Redmer in this mental and emotional tussle was, in my interpretation, central to the 'stay away permanently' position. They seem never to have stopped writing to each other, though he must have destroyed her letters — Did she keep his? Where are they now? — and they continued to dream, though fantasise is probably the better word, and probably more so on her side than his, about being together again.

I think that Bill filled the void in his life that was Mary, as representative of overseas adventure and success, by immersing himself in his work. That vast outpouring of research and writing, the frequent lectures, the relentless travel to any corner of New Zealand to speak on any aspect of the country's development, all this owed something to her absent presence in his mental life, and his constant, restless attempts, through displacement activity, to free himself from it. These activities may, for all I know, have included brief relationships with other women,[5] and he may also have seen Mary again, possibly on the few occasions when he was outside New Zealand, though he went abroad, and only on official business, very rarely between 1950 and his death. Most poignant of all, there is one letter from Mary to sister Shirley towards the end of the series in which she refers to Bill having promised to leave and go to her, I suspect in 1966. He certainly never did so.

In the early spring of 1968 Bill had a heart attack. Now that I am in my seventies, already nine years older than Bill when he died, I find it easy to imagine how he might have carried this forsaken love through most of the second half of his life, the daily waking dream of an alternative, a commitment dishonoured, a fulfilling physical relationship abandoned. I had seen it in other men. Even inside my own family in England. How much tension can a man of this sort endure?

If Bill destroyed her letters to him, how are we to know even this much? The answer is in the letters kept by sister Shirley. And they emphasise uncertainty in a way that might have wrecked anyone's fragile emotional world. Mary's letters clearly indicate that she was bisexual and that she had

61

had a love affair with sister Shirley in 1948 when the latter was in the United States, thanks to a grant from director of education Clarence Beeby, to research educational arrangements for disadvantaged children. Mary's letters to sister Shirley are quite clear about this, as they are about her relationship with Bill.

Using, perhaps, the cold, unimaginative eye of a journalist, one might say that brother and sister had shared Mary Redmer as a lover. But human relations are not so cold. The warmth, not to say intensity, of Mary's feelings for Bill don't seep, they pour from these letters. She was a woman of warmth, passion and intellect. It would be impossible not to recognise the importance that he held for her.

In the context of all that happened around that dinner table in the early 1970s, I believe that at some stage, perhaps in the course of heated discussion about my marriage to Helen, Shirley had shown her brother the letters. This was how he learned of his sister's lesbianism. This was how he learned of Mary's love for her, his own sister. And worst of all, this is how he learned of Mary's death, probably, as a letter from her husband suggests, by suicide. Suicide brought on by despair allied to depressive illness? And was this despair, in the end, prompted by Bill's failure to come to her? Perhaps he had written to say as much.

I think now that everything that happened to Bill in his last decade, from the loss in 1965 of his self-defining role as secretary of Industries and Commerce through to his death in 1975, was the culmination of this matter in his secret other life, a life he never confided, so far as I know, to anyone, but of which his sister had long since known. In such destructive circumstances, worthy of a modern Thomas Hardy, a man might decide that he didn't really care very much about anything any more. Knowledge of Bill's physical and mental condition in his final years brought into even sharper focus the cruelty of what was inflicted on him, by the SIS and its allies in various parts of the law and the public services, by much of the press and — let's be clear — by the Russian Embassy. But then these people knew no more than I did and were perhaps also ignorant of their own limitations.

I had no wish then to make Bill out a tragic figure. I have my own view of what might constitute betrayal. But we each have a duty to try to understand behaviour and not condemn it simply because it isn't ours, or doesn't conform to some pre-ordained assumption about what is and is not superior in human conduct. There is paradox and ambiguity in everyone. Certainly I feel now a more intense sorrow for Shirley. Helen's feelings about these discoveries, and my feelings for her as a result, I pass over in silence.

III

And so we come back, as always and ever, to the question: Was Bill Sutch a spy?

It is fruitless to pretend that he wasn't trying to meet and presumably talk to a member of the Russian Embassy in Wellington in the winter and spring of 1974. Furthermore, the action constituted — as the Chief Justice, Richard Wild, obligingly pointed out in December that year — a prima facie breach of the Official Secrets Act. Shirley herself, astute lawyer as she was, said to us privately at the time that this was perfectly, not to say abundantly, clear. This fact was in turn pointed out to the jury in the High Court in February 1975, but they found him not guilty even so. Bill didn't take the stand, so wasn't cross-examined, and relied for the most part on the strength of his reputation as a loyal and committed New Zealander to withstand the prosecution evidence.

Presumably the jury felt that this was strong enough proof of his innocence of wrongdoing and that to reach a different verdict they should at least have been told what the pair were talking *about*. But no one knew then and no one knows now. It may also be worth observing that the SIS of the 1960s and 1970s did not help itself in the matter of professionalism and impartiality. It was widely regarded as a risible, incompetent organisation, poorly led, administratively inflexible and intellectually dull as well as biased. An odd combination of the rigid and the limp. This would hardly have been lost on the jury, given the quality of the evidence and of the SIS officers who presented it at the trial.

And just in case it wasn't, Attorney-General Martyn Finlay, who had 'reluctantly' (his word) allowed the prosecution to proceed, thought, in October of 1974, and with some prescience, that 'what had the appearance of a melodrama might turn out to be a farce'. He amplified this in December when he said, in print, 'I tend to regard the Security Service in New Zealand as more stupid than dangerous. It wastes money and it wastes time.'[1] He went on to point out that the government of New Zealand had no permanent secrets and therefore no need of a security service.

Odder and odder. Bill, of course, had ceased to be a public servant nine years before this, so if he had government secrets to impart they must have been dead from the cold long since. The people who concluded that the whole exercise was a political manoeuvre designed to embarrass the government later came to see it as the first move in the manipulation of the 1975 election — dancing Cossacks and so forth. Bill Rowling, who at the time of Bill's arrest had only recently become prime minister after the sudden death of Norman Kirk, was bitter about the matter: he had been thinking of calling an early election to consolidate his position and the kerfuffle over Bill persuaded him against this. The election a year later brought about his political demise. I doubt he ever forgave Bill. Nor did many others.

The security establishment had three different consolidated suspicions about Bill's capacity to tell the Russians things they didn't ought to know, and they continued to air these in different contexts over the following years. One was that he was just one member of a ring of spies whose other members were still in the public service and for whom he was presumed to be a rapporteur or courier. They were said to have thought this on the night of his arrest and claimed that they initially proposed immunity for him if he cooperated. He declined, but then the idea in itself was silly.

The second was that he had had meetings with a KGB officer throughout the 1960s, but that the Russian concerned had been so skilful that they had never been able to catch the pair of them at it.[2] The third was that Bill did know some secret contemporary matters because he had, unofficially, been advising Norman Kirk on future economic and financial policy. No one, to my knowledge, ever got to the bottom of this assertion, though there were enough cold warriors in the press corps to keep it alive, if not actually kicking, for a few years after the event.[3]

These suppositions always seemed pretty thin to me, bearing out Martyn Finlay's dismissive view. Their thinness was brought into slightly better focus in 2008 when the minister responsible for the SIS, Helen Clark, authorised the release of Bill's security file to the public. As is normal in such cases, some material had been redacted, so we still don't know what the whole file may have contained. And nor do we know the extent to which it may have been doctored not just by deletions but by additions. Always a consideration to be borne in mind in such cases.[4] The two items from the file reproduced at the end of this book illustrate its quality well enough.

My view, still unchanged, is that the file added nothing to what we already knew, either about Bill, or about the SIS's suspicions or methods during the post-war years of its operation under the flawed act. Because it added no clear factual evidence to what was already known, the release of the file made no difference to the thinking of those who had a view, either for or against the idea of Bill as a spy. In general, however, media reception tended towards the 'no case to answer' interpretation.

Two large questions suggest themselves in the wake of the experiences I have tried to capture in this memoir. One is about the place, role and function of security services during the Cold War. The other has to do with the meaning of the word 'spy' in the context of a life such as Bill's. Of his 68 years, 10 were lived under conditions of hot war, 10 more in the Great Depression and 28 under Cold War conditions. The political catastrophes of his age included the military and political disasters of the First World War, the revolutions and economic crises that followed it, the rise of fascism, the murder of European Jewry, the long, long wars of China, Japan and Vietnam and the catastrophic destruction of central, southern and western Europe. Turbulence, loss, misery.

The Cold War, spanning the years from 1947 to 1991 — from roughly the Soviet rejection of the Marshall Plan through to the collapse of the USSR — was fought on a number of different fronts. Military competition for strategic dominance gave way eventually to the acceptance on both sides of the theory of mutually assured destruction (MAD — a good enough descriptor for the whole enterprise, you might say). Then there was economic conflict alongside hot wars in colonial and post-colonial settings, all accompanied by fierce diplomatic competition in both bi- and multilateral settings. And overarching all of this, cultural competition masking propaganda with everything from ballet to popular culture, and among it all the secret, dangerous world of espionage and counter-espionage.

The more one discovers about the last of these sectors, the more absurd it appears to have been. Many of the people at the helm of security endeavours worldwide seem to have been unbalanced: J. Edgar Hoover and James Jesus Angleton in the United States; men like Anthony Blunt, Kim Philby and Peter Wright in Britain; and more or less anyone at the head of the KGB or the East German Stasi. All of them seem to have been politically motivated by ideas of loyalty to their various governments that left much to be desired, particularly in the realm of the liberty of the citizen.

Many billions of roubles and dollars must have been expended throughout the world in the running of agents, the search for enemy agents, the surveillance of their own societies in the search for traitors, the implementation of domestic policies of repression out of a paranoid belief that the administration of government — Soviet or British, Polish or Indian, French or Italian — was at risk from subversive elements. And so on.

None of this expensive energetic pursuit of unrealisable objectives produced, as far as I have been able to tell, much that was of use. It is no longer unreasonable to believe that secrets supposedly made available by spies to the 'other' side made little difference to the arms or any other strategic race. The truth was far more prosaic. Close monitoring of technical and military journals, along with available electronic and telephonic surveillance, were the less romantic but ultimately successful methods by which each side kept abreast of the other.

To put it more starkly, if no agents had been run, their betrayal would not have been possible. Had there been no security apparatus into which to recruit potentially insecure individuals, they would not have been in a position to betray it. The world of security services contributed next to nothing to the outcome of the Cold War other than to sow suspicion and create unjustified anxiety.

The bigger truth surely is that the security services of both sides were really in an alliance of hostilities with each other rather than protecting their own citizens; ever eager to expand their budgets in the search for proof of their Cold War utility and their fantastical objectives; mirrors reflecting mirrors, reflecting yet more distorting mirrors. The KGB and the CIA, along with all the sharks and minnows that swam with and against them, were really in an alliance of their own. Like some malign international sporting league, playing a deadly game that degenerated into the punishment of their own citizens, while signals and electronic intelligence on the one hand, and serious library research on the other, delivered such information as governments believed they needed.

The harm that secret security intelligence services did far outweighed any productive good, and the damage that they inflicted was more or less entirely on their own citizens. The broad understanding of the role and function of, for instance, the Stasi that has come to light since the reunification of Germany is more than indicative. Wrecked careers, ruined opportunities, wasted resources, lost lives, distorted politics: future historical judgement will see these as the principal outcomes.[5]

I t is easy to see Bill as a victim of this nonsense. But it is important to understand, at the same time, that he was never a passive victim. As Shirley often remarked, he was incorrigibly independent of influence, careless of prohibitions, stubbornly determined to do whatever he wanted to do. Nothing would divert him from a course of action he thought right. If there were people he wanted to talk to, he would seek them out and talk to them. She also confided to us that he was impossible to argue with because once he had made up his mind about something he was disinclined ever to change it. He simply followed his own judgement. Others could follow him if they wished; should follow him if they were to be considered what he thought of as sensible. He seemed to have no sense that his own opinion might ever be faulty.

Shirley knew him better than any of us, but the idea of him as intransigent in this way wasn't, I think, quite right. Certainly he was strong minded. And he definitely held views on a small number of historical subjects that could be contentious. Red rags to conservative bulls. He was, for instance, immovable on the subject of the Spanish Civil War, where he sided intellectually and emotionally with the Republican cause and sought many opportunities to say so. I've never been able to see much wrong with that. He detested fascism in all the forms that it took in the 1920s and 1930s and he probably felt as strongly about this as Winston Churchill. He believed, correctly in military terms, that the Russian army, first at the Battle of Stalingrad, and subsequently in the advance on Berlin, had been the main cause of Germany's total defeat in the Second World War. They had been welcomed as allies then. He was opposed to their demonisation in the post-war world.

But he could change his mind on some things. He gave way over some aspects of the design of the Brooklyn house that Shirley really insisted on. Similarly, some of his behaviour over the final year or two of our relationship suggested that he had changed his mind about my presence at the table as his son-in-law. He appeared, too, to have changed his views about the role of women in society years

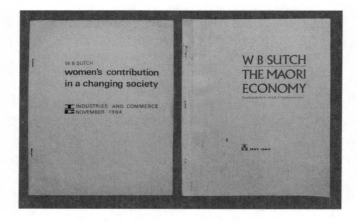

Two examples of the immense number of official reports
from the Department of Industries and Commerce, both
published in 1964. A torrent of publications, leaving
opponents flat-footed, dumbfounded, outmanoeuvred
and intellectually drained.

before I met him, from his early conventional outlook to his later advocacy of their interests. He had definitely altered his view about the propriety of his meetings with Razgovorov.

Most important of all, for those who care for the human side of relationships, the enduring qualities of understanding and affection that lie at the roots of being, we learned that he talked frankly and honestly to Shirley over two days in Wellington hospital before he went into a final coma. Shirley never reported to me what they said to each other, but I do know that she was deeply grateful to have had those hours, and she wrote to thank the medical staff for permitting them the privacy to talk in this way. She was immensely buoyed by the things that he told her and the knowledge of the bonds that held them so closely together. It greatly helped her to come through the inevitable publicity of Bill's funeral and its aftermath and it was to be one of the springboards, much later, to her reassessment of her own life alongside his.

Was the stubborn intransigence of Shirley's recollection the stuff of which spies are made? Bill could be wonderfully eccentric by some standards. Hugh Price reported that he and some friends, young students — this would have been in the early 1950s — asked to visit Bill at home to talk about contemporary society. He agreed, but then devoted the entire evening to playing them folk chants from his Smithsonian record collection of tribal music. Ethnography in practice. It was, presumably, an interest derived from his devotion to the anthropological approach to art from his reading of Boas, but coming soon after the waterfront lockout of 1951, and their own experience of the stupidity of the SIS — they had been subjected to surveillance for reprinting articles about international affairs from, unbelievably, the *Times*, the *Washington Post* and the *Manchester Guardian*[6] — it filled these young men with perplexed chagrin.

Stubborn, eccentric, wayward. When Bill died the *Dominion* called him 'Our Stormy Petrel'. The 'spy' label persisted, of course, and for a few years intensified, as it suited various parts of our small society to denigrate his reputation. Robert Muldoon, prime minister to New Zealanders in their bullish mode, and whom all New Zealanders knew to have been touched by Circe long since, said Bill was 'as guilty as sin', a cliché that he appeared to believe was original (so to speak). The line had actually been given to him by senior public servant Gerald Hensley,[7] who reports having done so in his delightful memoirs, where so often, and in the great tradition of *Yes Minister*, he has his cake and eats it too. Whim Wham gave Muldoon and Hensley a dry response in an eight-stanza poem published in various newspapers on 11 February 1980. It concludes:

> *He's dead, and will not answer,*
> *Nor cares how We behave,*
> *Nor stirs when urchin Fingers make*
> *Mud Pies upon his Grave.*[8]

All of this, from the importance, if any, of the role of security services in the Cold War, to the meaning of the term 'spy', to the harm inflicted on individuals by hidden judgements reached through surveillance regimes, were returned to the surface of public debate by the 1992 testimony of a Russian defector called Vasili Mitrokhin. According to this source, someone corresponding to a possible description of Bill was recruited by Russian intelligence in New York in 1950. His cover name was 'Maori' (oh dear, oh dear) but the archive that Mitrokhin brought with him to Britain via Latvia in 1992 did not name him, and the reference to 'Maori' is confined to a one-sentence entry in the published material.

There are a lot of interesting aspects to the Mitrokhin archive. He had seven suitcases full of parts of KGB files that he had copied by hand in the course of his work as KGB archivist and taken home from the office in his shoes. He is said to have offered this material to the Americans first, but they declined it, supposedly because the CIA did not trust him. They feared he was a plant and the material disinformation. This was probably the last lingering effect of Angleton's influence in the CIA, though he had died long since. But this is not to say that the rejection wasn't well founded. What led them to be suspicious we do not know.

The British, unlike the Americans, welcomed Mitrokhin and enabled the publication of two volumes of his archive, one dealing with the Western alliance and the other with the rest of the world.[9] In them he identifies and names many individuals as spies. Most of the names revealed in Britain were already well known, not just to MI5 but to the public, and so were confirmation of past dirty washing. However, Mitrokhin had apparently brought evidence of two spies supposedly previously unknown to the British security services: Melita Norwood and John Symonds. Somehow their names were leaked to the press and in the British summer of 1999 they were the subject of a television documentary and newspaper exposure. In these circumstances the first volume of Mitrokhin's revelations was published and a parliamentary committee asked to investigate and report on how his information had been handled.

My own reaction to these developments was one of relief on Shirley's behalf that there was no mention of either Bill or New Zealand in any of the material. She had suffered more than enough by this time, was growing old — she was 84 at the turn of the century — and could hardly have borne yet more controversy about her husband.

Nevertheless, the Mitrokhin papers proved easy to assimilate into my developing view of Cold War espionage. The parliamentary report distinguished between what it called 'agents' and 'confidential contacts'. In addition to the two named supposed agents working for the KGB in Britain, Mitrokhin identified a number of confidential contacts, whose names also made brief headlines in the newspapers. In defiance of the kind of witch-hunt of these supposed derelicts that any Cold War observer like me had come to expect, one of them — his name is of no importance now — simply issued a statement saying (I paraphrase): 'Yes, I was an active member of the Campaign for Nuclear Disarmament and still am. As a free citizen in a democracy I can and will talk to whomever I like about this matter, and that includes now and in the past, any Russian who would like to listen. So get lost.' The controversy dissolved immediately. Fair enough, I thought, though I also interpreted his statement to be rather different, so much was the climate changing, from what he might have had to say had his name been revealed, let us say, 25 years earlier.

The other really interesting aspect to this first phase of Mitrokhin enthusiasm was the fact that neither Norwood nor Symonds was ever charged with any offence under official secrets legislation. This seemed odd not only to observers like me, but to members of the British establishment. Much of the parliamentary committee report is devoted to this issue,[10] but despite their best endeavours it is clear that they never got to the bottom of it.

It was clear that, in Norwood's case, the security service pre-empted the role of the solicitor-general, making it impossible for a prosecution to proceed, and that Symonds had already, some years before Mitrokhin's arrival on the scene, been given immunity from prosecution. The committee huffs and puffs in its report, but is unable to give a convincing answer as to why the cases were handled in this way. One is left with the impression that the security services were a law unto themselves. The report states, reassuringly, that the problems of control have been remedied.

Security documentation, as both the report and the Mitrokhin publications themselves eloquently testify, always poses analytical problems. As one historian has recently observed, 'in no other discipline is the researcher "confronted with evidence precisely managed by their subject" — for the processing of official records for preservation in The National Archives, declassification or destruction offers government departments the means to massage, even to excise the narrative of their more secret activities.'[11]

Mitrokhin died in his bed in 2004, a privilege not generally accorded to members of the KGB who defect. The material he brought with him to the West has generally been received in different countries as truthful by many of the same members of the press who, in other contexts, would be unlikely to believe anything said by any member of the KGB, whether a defector or not. Much of the first volume of the archive recounted things that everyone already knew to be true; a little of the rest revealed a truth or two about previously unheard of collaborators. It was all very past history. One purpose of security intelligence services is to spread disinformation. Truths told can be designed as distractions from larger concerns. Why should this case be any different? I have long believed that the reasonable position is scepticism. We have been lied to too often.

But what is 'spy', outside the fantasy world of the movies, other than a term of particularly dishonourable condemnation? The problem for Russian diplomats throughout the Cold War was that no one in the West would talk to them. (When Pik Botha, apartheid South Africa's foreign minister from 1977 to 1994, was thought by hardliners in his own Afrikaner National Party to be a Soviet spy, his response was that, at diplomatic cocktail parties abroad, 'nobody would talk to us and nobody would talk to the Russians, so we ended up always having to talk to each other'.)[12] The normal avenues of diplomatic work were mainly closed and they were forbidden to travel around the Western countries in which they served. What was true for them was also true, though to a far lesser extent, for Western diplomats serving in Russia and the Warsaw Pact countries of Central Europe. So great was the suspicion and the prohibition that it was difficult to find interlocutors, let alone well-informed, intelligent ones.

This was one reason why Paddy Costello, when chargé d'affaires in the New Zealand legation in Moscow after the war, fell under suspicion by Western authorities. It was because of his skill at befriending people, particularly in the field of literature, so that they would talk to him. He went out of his way to meet them. As a result he was able to form shrewder judgements about Soviet military and other plans than other Western embassies could achieve. The access enabled him to report incidents to Wellington that meant we were better informed about Russia than either London or Washington, but the material seemed privileged and this made him an object of suspicion. And the insights he supplied were not trusted.

Members of the KGB had a further problem of their own, particularly during what Tony Judt called 'the frosty two cultures' stand off' from 1947 until the deaths of Joseph Stalin and Lavrentiy Beria in 1953.[13] This was the matter of their own fears. They were sent abroad to find and exploit sources of information. I have tried to imagine myself a KGB operative instructed to recruit informants in, let us say, the United States. You would know only too well the consequences of failure, whether real or imagined.[14] It could be at best career damaging, at worst life threatening. Unsurprisingly, these officials were eager to supply the names of those to whom they talked at functions, receptions, UN forums and other such places. As a result, all sorts of people turn up in files in the KGB archives, many erroneously listed as agents or confidential contacts, helpers or sources.

Even some hardened partisans among the Cold War triumphalists of the recent past recognise that the sweeping condemnation implied in the word 'spy' can be misplaced. As Herbert Romerstein has written, 'It is a little unfair . . . to simply refer to those controlled by Soviet intelligence as "spies" since they were not so much agents as contacts, or interpreters of political life, or perhaps, I suppose, just plain gossips.'[15] We've all known plenty of those. They may be mistaken, but they're not criminal. Bill was, apparently, talking to a Russian. Was that spying?

Over the years opinion about Bill as a 'spy' has evolved into two quite clear and distinct narratives. On the one hand is what can conveniently be called the past SIS account, in which Bill is the weasel. He was insufferably self-confident (Tararua in 1933); a braggart (the long walk from the Arctic Circle); a betrayer (first wife, second wife, confidential information at private government meetings); self-serving (avoidance of active service in the Second World War); miserly and too rich (house, artworks, drinks cupboard); Russian sympathiser and agent (signed up in the 1930s, if not then, then in southern Europe in 1946, if not then, then 1950); disobedient (record as a public servant); careless of obligations (books and articles published without authorisation); finally caught in the act (arrest and trial); and liar (post-trial public statements and income tax 'evasion'). The wartime accusation was a particularly unpleasant smear. Although he did not serve overseas, he went where directed — he became a gunnery instructor — and did as he was required to do. He may, yet again, have betrayed himself here by his tendency to brag, to prove himself cleverer than the authorities.

The finest account of the weasel narrative that I have seen all in one place is in Sir John Marshall's second volume of memoirs.[16] A very well-written few pages suggest some heavy dependence on SIS allegations (which as prime minister, very briefly, he would have been entitled to seek) and a carefully drafted assessment of Bill's character of apparently Olympian impartiality. It read very well when it was published, but time and history are unkind to the self-serving memoirs of disappointed politicians. Marshall had been Bill's minister from 1960, and the dismantling of his departmental secretary five years later smacks of his own difficult political situation. His writing suggests that he doth protest too much in denying the accusation that he was instrumental in Bill's dismissal.

His blanket assertion that Bill was mistrusted by the business community is unsupported. There is much evidence to show that he was enthusiastically supported by industrialists seeking to expand their role in the New Zealand economy, and strongly opposed by some parts of the pastoral sector, the heartland of National Party support. The statement that Bill was disliked by his ministry colleagues seems especially odd in the context of their many expressions of support and their dismay when his contract was not renewed. And Marshall's assessment of Bill's 'character' seems to lean heavily on the two unattributed and rather unpleasant SIS assessments which I reproduce in Appendix B at the end of this book. Still, as a summary of the Bill-as-weasel position, it remains one of the best we have.[17]

L et us point the question elsewhere. Why was it, and why is it still in some circles, so important for some people to label Bill a 'spy'? It seems fairly reasonable to state that he was never a traitor to New Zealand's interests, given the extent and focus of his life's work, and as for spying, to make the epithet fit Bill requires a rather more flexible meaning of the term than his detractors want to imply. (If he was talking to the Russians about New Zealand in the way that he used to talk to me at that time, good luck to them, because their general knowledge, perhaps even detailed knowledge, of the country would have been greatly improved.) I don't think it can be because of some elevated juridical understanding of the obligation of the subject to show allegiance to the Crown, since I don't recall this sort of thing ever turning up in the media or in the nasty anonymous mail that filled Shirley's letterbox.

And it hardly seems credible that it could be a judgement based on general ethical grounds, given the prevalence among Bill's fellow citizens, both those with positions of power and those of lesser status, to produce illegitimate babies, treat their spouses with disrespect, drink to excess, mistreat and abuse their children, negotiate suspect business contracts, betray creditors in bankruptcy cases and be economical with the truth in politics. One might be tempted to describe accusations from these quarters as throwing the first stone from inside a glasshouse.

Being able to stick the spy label on Bill is rather more understandable in the case of the SIS. He could serve as justification for all their past dreary messes. In this he became their get-out-of-jail-card, so they were disinclined to let him go, even though he had been acquitted in a court of law that, as guardians of the integrity of the democratic state under the rule of law, they were committed to upholding. The fact that they saw themselves as free of this obligation indicates their need for Bill to be the spy they wanted him to be. It was hard work, but they stuck to it manfully.

My own view now is that their era has waned. Retirement and the great reaper do history's work, contributing to a reshaping of the past that can disfigure the bland face of previous assumptions about the truth. The Cold War waged by and between security services is what now seems increasingly deviant, from MI5's old-boy network method of recruitment with its disastrous consequences, through to KGB and FBI stigmatisation of Jews and dissenters. In recent years our own security services, much reformed, appear to be staffed by better qualified recruits, who owe nothing to the service's Cold War past and have altogether other and different security problems on which to focus. It may even be possible to believe that a more professional service has come into being. We shall see.

Time has also opened eyes to the power of rhetoric in political life. George Orwell's 1984, with its 'newspeak' and inversions of meaning, is now widely used as a school text. Everyone knows that if you can persuade people that they are at war then you can persuade them of the need for limitations on their freedoms, constraints on their liberty, intrusions into and surveillance of their affairs and demands on their movements and allegiances. Governments learned this well during the Second World War. They amply employed the knowledge throughout the Cold War, which wasn't of course a war at all, not a real war, at least not outside the unfortunate border and colonial territories where sabre rattlers were privileged to draw and use their weapons.

The rhetorical uses of war as a device for securing compliance are never lost on the powerful: Why else have we been encouraged to embrace a war on drugs and a war on terror? I don't think Bill believed in the Cold War. He saw it for what it was, the rhetoric of political orthodoxies. If this is a war then there must be allies and enemies, belligerents and non-combatants, battlegrounds and strategies, victories and defeats. Casualties are inevitable, regrettable of course, but necessary if 'we' are to 'win'. Conscientious objection is punishable by vilification and abuse; the crossing of borders is treachery; talking, betrayal.

A man of Bill's independence of mind would have thought this nonsensical and inhuman. His experience of it all around him in the New York of the late 1940s would have both sickened and disheartened him. It is tempting to hear his voice, in the world of today, pointing out what the rhetoric has done. Declarations of 'victory' in the Cold War have helped to bring about the new corporate criminality of contemporary Russia, bitter over its 'humiliation' in 'defeat'. In politics you reap in substance what you sow in rhetoric.

But away from the security service of the second half of the twentieth century the reasons for Bill's value to a certain kind of opinion as 'spy' seem to me psychological. Here he can serve as a relief valve for that sense of semi-educated bourgeois propriety that, stuffed with rectitude and right thinking, impervious to the nuance and ambiguity of others' circumstances, fuels its daily life with the stale fodder of received opinion. Conservative in outlook, such people are never really happy to examine either themselves or the world around them with a steady and unflinching gaze. They knew little, and cared less for Bill's many achievements, had no real sense of the historical circumstances of his birth, upbringing or young manhood and effectively no sympathy for the life of the mind that he and many of his contemporaries lived. They were then, and in a few cases I think still are today, ready to be persuaded by the convenient label of weasel.

These are, of course, our fellow citizens, our equals in the arena of public life, and it is reasonable to believe, as I do, that Bill was negligent in failing to recognise them not only as a threat to his understanding of what it meant to be a New Zealander, but also as a mortal danger to him if he were ever to overstep the mark drawn for them in the sand by their elected political masters. The tragedy of Bill's life is that for them the journey matters little. Only the arrival. Only the last day. Everything else falls under the shadow of his final months. All is to be defined by its dying moments.

For many other people, however, Bill's last days, his arrival, mattered little in the context of what preceded it. They treated his acquittal at the trial as completely justified and a cause for celebration. Telegrams, cards and letters poured in from all round the country. The people who sent them, and many with whom I have discussed the topic over the more than 40 years since, have sought to wave the trial away as an absurdity, which I fear it never was. Some saw him simply as impish, like the young man who hadn't been lost, and hadn't been found in the Tararua Range. He was an original, he didn't give a fig — a sort of she'll be right New Zealand nonchalance writ large. And as it happens he was a bit of a fan of Barry Crump and warmly recommended his books to me.

Others held Bill dear as a courageous risk taker, pointing with evident pleasure to the possibility that he had leaked information to radical journalist Claud Cockburn about New Zealand's differences with Britain over Japanese militarism at a meeting in London in 1937. This may have been New Zealand's first expression of a foreign policy independent of the mother country and giving it to the press was just the kind of thing that Bill might do. The British security service minuted that they thought it was him and he was marked down as unreliable.[18] British foreign policy in the 1930s is now widely seen as treacherous and pusillanimous. By 1975, New Zealanders regarded a disobliging refusal to toe the British line in the 1930s as liberating. This sort of risk taking, they thought, applied to Bill throughout his career. It brought him down in the end, but had been worth it even so. As I have frequently reflected, other people's severe pain is always easier to bear than your own.

Some, however, simply loved the adventure in the man, the extraordinary movement and diversity of his experience. They applauded his role at the UN in organising the vote to ensure the survival of the United Nations Children's Fund, UNICEF, when it was American policy to close it. They were impressed by his role at United Nations Relief and Rehabilitation Administration, first in arranging supplies for the Asian region out of an office in Sydney in 1945, subsequently by the reports that he originated about the needs of those in the devastated regions of Europe, especially in the Balkans in 1946.

They also saw his outspoken support for unpopular causes as yet more evidence of his adventurous spirit: trade with Indonesia, support for domestic industries, diversification of the economy away from too great a reliance on primary produce, high standards of design, consumer protection, warnings of our vulnerability from British membership of what would become the European Union, care for the environment, heritage conservation in the cities, town and public transport planning, equality for women — the list is long. Who disagrees with these positions today? In the 1950s and 1960s they were the sign of a bold dissenter and therefore appealed to many people who felt they had a spokesman on the inside. We barely need reminding of the saying about prophets in their own country.

Others who had heard him lecture, or read one or other of his history books, admired his clarity of thought, his grasp of complex material and his obvious devotion to the welfare of his own country and its people. In 2007 I spoke at an Alexander Turnbull Library exhibition of the posters that Bill had collected in Europe during the 1930s and through the war years: *Towards the Precipice — Propaganda Posters*. During question and answer time a woman in the audience described going to hear Bill speak one evening. She was a potter, and, knowing that he took an interest in the Studio Pottery movement and had sought to have the Department of Industries and Commerce support them, she spoke to him afterwards about her difficulties in Taranaki, where she lived. She was astonished when Bill proceeded to explain to her the variety of minerals and other deposits in the Taranaki subsoil, their precise locations, and their efficacy for making different types of slips and glazes. This was all offered to her in the kindest and most helpful way. Forty years later she had never forgotten. Hardly surprising.

Among those who knew him personally, almost all of those I have met saw him as an honest man who had devoted his working life to trying to improve the lot of his fellow New Zealanders. For them, the evidence of his loyalty was so immense that they couldn't believe that the events of the last year of his life had any conceivable importance. They interpreted his conduct throughout the trial, calm, impassive, scrupulously polite, as an object lesson in how to respond to persecution.[19] For those who saw things in this way, Bill was a lion. For them it was unquestionably his life's work that mattered. Where the fates set him down at the end was irrelevant.

I don't know much about the fates myself. Bill did, however, perform with the KGB and the SIS in the silly two-step dance that they were playing and he paid a very heavy price for it. He left behind a mess of accusations and of personal hurt that his family has had to live with ever after. There was, and still is, little solace in seeking intellectual justification for his waywardness. That was who he was. As a man of the world, let loose in the world, he enjoyed his life, making of it what he wanted.

There is much to be said for living in this way. Many artists and writers achieve such an independent existence, and their sins and betrayals are forgiven, or passed over, because they seem somehow to deserve, through the product of their labours, a latitude not extended to the rest of us. But this posthumous liberty is denied the man to whom the label 'spy' might be attached, even in defiance of his acquittal. For some reason it has always been open season for Bill-hunters. Essayists, would-be biographers, television documentary-makers, no doubt eventually playwrights or film-makers, must line up to add to the burdens of bad taste and distortion that those who knew him well have had to bear. No one has suffered more from this than Helen, my wife of all these years, who knew of her father's love and has responded to it with poised and eloquent loyalty throughout her life.

The freedom that Bill achieved struck me as fitting his appearance. He was a sliver under six feet tall, erect and slim. He had had a fine head of hair as a young man and he set it off with the thin moustache made popular in the 1930s by

The handsome gunnery instructor aged 36 or 37.

Errol Flynn, Clark Gable and others. Someone told me that 'the Sutch boys', Bill and his younger brother Ted, gave easily the best parties in Wellington in the 1930s.

His hair thinned as he aged, with very little of it left by the time I met him, but he always kept the moustache. It reminded me of our next-door neighbour when I was a very small boy. He was called Mr Patten and he 'travelled in leather goods'. I could never quite get this image out of my mind whenever I saw Bill. In a way, Bill travelled in New Zealand history and New Zealand development and the ideas that he believed went with them, spreading them around him, urging others to pick them up. A lot of these ideas were about administration in one way or another, many more about design and social cohesion, others imperialism, colonialism and its effects, and others, central to all else, about the importance of people. These are what he gave out.

What he took in, as anyone travelling in goods of one sort of another must, was a yearning for the good opinion of whoever he was with, for reassurance about his importance in the world: for security.

If only,
if only . . .

A memoir of Shirley Smith

Two incidents 56 years apart.

We are on the platform of Warsaw railway station, high European summer, 1998. Shirley, 81 years old, has been staying with us at our home in Konstancin-Jeziorna, a pleasant residential neighbourhood some 30 minutes from the centre of the city, and we have driven her in to catch a train to Germany. She is eager to revisit the cathedral in Frankfurt, not seen since her days of European travel from Oxford in the second half of the 1930s. After that she will go on to stay with friends of ours in Brussels.

The train is one of those ancient Central European models that we now see only in films. The door sits high above its carriage bogies like something out of a novel by Czech writer Bohumil Hrabal. There are steep steps to climb to board the carriage, a wide gap between platform and steps and a deep concrete drop to the rails far below. Crispin, our athletically fit younger son, visiting in his summer vacation from university in England, has her suitcase in one hand. 'Shirley,' I say, 'wait while I get onto the train and then we can help you up the steps. They . . .'

I get no further. Determined to embark in her own way,

Shirley launches herself at the steps, misses her footing, slips and starts to fall onto the rails through the gap between platform and train. Shrieks, turned heads, the rise of sickening fear. Crispin reaches out and with one hand grabs her by the wrist, has her suspended over the drop for half a second, then hauls her back to safety. She is unhurt. The other three of us feel in need of a sedative. We regroup before I get on the train and hand her up.

June, 1942. Shirley has had Bill to stay for a weekend in Auckland, where she is teaching classics at the University College. Among his clothes to be washed before he leaves are some of those collars men wore in those days, detachable from the body of the shirt and requiring to be starched. Bill expects Shirley to do the wash and starch because in the working-class household from which he comes that is woman's work. Shirley is appalled. She had grown up in a home with a housekeeper; she had attended private boarding school and then been an undergraduate in an Oxford college in the days when college servants, known as scouts, did everything for you. She didn't know how to starch a collar and as an independent professional woman had no intention of learning now. If women did this sort of work, she wasn't one of them. Bill elected the easier course and gave up wearing stiff collars. Shirley told me this story herself.

Impetuous. Impulsive. Stubborn. They can also be seen as parts of the package we call courage, or its near cousin, audacity. Ever since French Revolutionary hero Georges Danton and his famous slogan, *'De l'audace! Encore de l'audace! Toujours de l'audace!'*, we have been encouraged to think well of the audacious, but it doesn't always work to your advantage. It may give cause for regret. If only, if only . . .

Shirley was small. Five foot nothing. Actually a few inches more than that, but it was the first thing that I noticed about her, standing on the deck of the houseboat Helen had rented for a few weeks at the end of the 1970 Oxford summer term when the lease on her flat was soon to expire. Seen from the riverbank, Shirley exuded a kind of diminutive, restrained displeasure, as though she had rather hoped that I wouldn't turn up. I very quickly discovered her to be a tough customer, sure of what she wanted and determined in how she went about trying to secure it. Had she been a man, people would perhaps have said she had a Napoleon complex — that peculiarly gender-loaded put-down applied to short men with strong personalities. Oh, we all know about them. They're making up for their sense of inferiority.

I wasn't intimidated, but I was perplexed. Shirley didn't need to prove anything to me. She was the mother of the young woman I was in love with, so she already had a lot going for her. And Helen had already prepared me with the background. Her mother hadn't been away from New Zealand since 1950, so this was a long yearned for and imagined trip. It was 20 years since she returned to Wellington from New York with her five-year-old daughter, her budding wartime career as a university classics lecturer six years lost behind her and her future as anything other than housewife remote and uncertain.

In those two decades she had found a way to combine motherhood with university law studies, helped her husband to build, equip and move into a new home, taught Roman law and constitutional law to undergraduates, edited the *New Zealand Law Journal*, served a clerkship in a Wellington law firm and then set up a thriving sole practice as a barrister and solicitor.

She was a founder of the New Zealand Civil Liberties Union, served the Wellington Cook Island community — especially its women — as pro bono legal adviser, assisted in the creation and establishment of the regulations that preserved as heritage what remained of the inner-city suburb of Thorndon after the building of the motorway, was lawyer to the Women's Electoral Lobby, helped to secure and then endow the Rita Angus cottage, was among those leading the 'No Maoris, No Tour' protests over rugby contact with apartheid South Africa, played a similar leadership role in the 'Save Manapouri' campaign and had been national secretary of the New Zealand Campaign for Nuclear Disarmament, while all the time acting as cook and hostess for her husband's rising career.

Knowing the facts is very different from knowing what a life of service lived in this way must have entailed, and as is common with young people, who inevitably lack experience — which is what it means to be young — I had no conception of the hard work and endurance required. I was to watch it with admiration, not to say amazement, over much of the ensuing 30 years: the volume of legal business mail that flowed from her pen and typewriter; the trips to the office at 2 a.m. of a Sunday with the vacuum cleaner to smarten the place up before the coming week's work; the time and effort devoted to what looked to me like lame ducks, hopeless cases or undeserving tricksters because everyone deserved to be heard, everyone was entitled to legal representation, everyone was equal before the law. She was a sort of one woman crusader on the side of the public interest. Sometimes it was tiring just to watch. You couldn't but admire the determination.

Where had it come from?

The first narrative I developed about Shirley was one of privilege. Her father, Sir David Smith, born in

New Zealand in 1888 to Scottish Presbyterians from Aberdeen, had made his way in the law, was already a widely respected and successful barrister in Wellington by the time Shirley was born in 1916, was the youngest appointment to the Supreme Court in 1928, and after retiring from the bench in 1948 went on to be chairman of the Board of Trade and the last chancellor of the University of New Zealand before it was divided into four independent universities. Shirley grew up in a house where there was always at least one servant. She was educated at private schools: Queen Margaret and Auckland Diocesan as a day girl and then as a boarder at Nga Tawa near the little Manawatū town of Marton, where she had excellent tuition in Latin and Greek, enabling her to pass the general entrance examination for Oxford. She went up as an 18-year-old commoner (i.e. not the holder of a scholarship or exhibition) to St Hugh's College in October 1935 to study classical languages and literature and philosophy. For her four years in Oxford she lived in college, with a scout to clean and service her room, and never had to do her own laundry or cooking.

I reckoned I knew what an upbringing of this kind meant because I had been able to observe it, by contrast and comparison, among my contemporaries in England. My own family, both sides, had come out of the East End of London. Schools for us were public, crowded (there were 40 or so children in my primary school class), not always particularly well taught and organised through discipline, rote learning and punishment. Progress in education was defined and structured by examinations — 11-plus, O levels, A levels — and scholarships, if you were judged good enough to land one.

Between the ages of 10 and 24, when I arrived at Nuffield College, Oxford to start work on a doctoral thesis, I had sat seven separate public examinations designed to sort us into tiers of merit (or not) and provide sufficient financial reward to proceed to the next level. I had no resentments about this. I thought of myself as incredibly lucky and, as it happened, the further you went through this arduous system the more attention was paid to you as someone succeeding on merit, as opposed to by wealth and association. This attention brought its own substantial rewards.

Our contemporaries who went to public, mainly boarding schools, had small classes, individual attention, longer hours of instruction, all the extraordinary benefits of playing fields and sports coaching and, as often as not, private scholarships to selected colleges at Oxford and Cambridge. Unsurprisingly they swanned through, our expression, to occupy the majority of university places; places that were available, when I matriculated in 1962, to only 4 or 5 per cent of the entire population of 18-year-olds. They also turned out very often to be the ones with heaps of self-confidence, who held advanced, and as often as not Marxist, opinions about the world. In short, they had the presumption that goes with being superior and privileged. Some segments of the English upper classes were very good at this. They played at politics as an elevated game, divorced from the world of practical experience. Like table tennis, or draw poker played for matches, pleasure and high seriousness could be enjoyed without risk.

I thought this was the Shirley I was meeting, and at first she did little to disabuse me or, if she tried, I simply didn't notice. She was immensely pleased to be back in Oxford, which she hadn't seen for nearly a quarter of a century; to make contact again with Dan and Winnie Davin, with whom she had spent many happy hours in 1946 when Bill was away on UNRRA duties in the Balkans; to meet Helen's economics tutors, Theo Cooper and David Soskice; and to be present at Helen's graduation ceremony in the Sheldonian Theatre, one of Christopher Wren's seventeenth-century gems and part of the grandeur of Oxford's architectural heritage that fitted snugly with Shirley's memories of her pre-war undergraduate life.

I didn't see much of this. It was post-examination time at the University of Essex and I was neck deep in script marking and board meetings, so my introduction to Shirley on the river, though followed by an evening in the Victoria Arms in the warm company of Dan Davin and his circle, was brief. I was soon back on the train to Colchester. I missed two indicative events. Helen had organised a little evening drinks party for her flatmates and friends, to say goodbye as they all headed off in different vacation directions and to give Shirley an opportunity to see where her daughter had been living and meet the people she knew.

Shirley swept into this occasion and was soon on some sort of Oxford high. She captivated — or at any rate captured — all the young women who were present with her stories of Oxford life in the 1930s, of the people she had known, the journeys she had made to Greece and to Germany, to Switzerland and to France, the politics of the time, the rules and regulations, college life, books and friendship. They sat in a circle around her. No one else joined in. She had the floor and she held it. The speck of awareness that she had locked her own daughter out of the pleasurable discourse of her own farewell party never troubled the smooth ointment of her own happiness.

This story, as told to me by Helen, saddened and exasperated, came back to mind often over the years. It held two truths. One was that Shirley loved a party. The other was that if you were giving one to include her, make sure you had enough people to break it into clusters. Shirley's love of partying, too little indulged in her life, remained with her until the end. When we gave a seventieth birthday party for her in 1986 she outlasted almost all of the 80 or so people who came, and was still ready for laughter over reminiscence and a 'last' (surely) glass of wine at two in the morning, by which time my own conviviality had long been exhausted.

The other Oxford event of this 1970 visit, also related to me by Helen, was of accompanying Shirley to lunch in Merton College at the invitation of Norman Davis. Here was another brilliant New Zealander of that gifted generation of 1930s scholars, by then an eminent professor of English, whom Shirley had known well when they were both undergraduates. Shirley confided to Helen that he had asked her to marry him, but friendship had never matured into love on her side. She had turned him down, but the flame he held for her never perished and flared up in the many letters they exchanged down the years. Shirley told us that after Bill died, and on another of her return visits to Oxford, Norman asked her again. His wife Lena had died in 1983. This time I think she was greatly tempted. Here was the real possibility of a completely new departure in life.

The knowledge of this intertwining of personal intimacies illuminated for me an entry, otherwise quite gnomic, in Dan Davin's diary for 13 August 1947: 'Last night [i.e. 12th] . . . ninish [sic] went off with W[innie] to Shirley's for coffee with her and Norman and Nina [sic] Davis. Norman uneasy and incapable of carrying off his situation with grace lapsed into his old boorishness.' Suggestive now, tempting interpretation after all these years. Shirley was still only 30 years old when Dan wrote this, just a few years after the rupture of the Second World War that took Norman to courageous undercover work in the Balkans. He was lecturing at the University of Sofia when war was declared in 1939. Recruited by the Special Operations Executive of

British intelligence, he served in both Bulgaria and Turkey for four years. Shirley had returned to New Zealand.

Oxford remained Shirley's spiritual home of the imagination. The visits to the city became more frequent after that 1970 return. She was there again in 1981, when Helen and I had gone to live in Paris and she was able to visit. And again in 1984, when we also went to Crete together, and once more in 1987. She was immensely proud that both her daughter and her younger grandson also studied at St Hugh's and barely minded at all that her other grandson went to Somerville College instead. Both young men were able to dine with us when we celebrated Shirley's eightieth birthday in Oxford in 1996; her happiness then still lives rich in the memory.

On one occasion she stayed with Norman and again was a guest at the Merton high table. She loved such small rituals of civilised living and took great pleasure in attending gaudies at St Hugh's, developing an ever stronger affection for the college and the wealth of experience towards which it had steered her so long before. She had a fine indignant distaste for James McNeish's *Dance of the Peacocks*, that it told stories only of men.[1] Somehow he seemed to have missed the interesting New Zealand women at Oxford in the 1930s who had gone on to do a few big things in the world.

Refusing Norman Davis' second proposal, with its promise of security and company among intellectuals she admired, in a city she adored, was a sign perhaps that she knew Oxford could now only be a romantic fantasy, one she might indulge in at a distance, or actually embrace for a few days every few years, but not one to replace the reality of her home life in Wellington, solitary as her domesticity had become. She may, however, have been brought to this realisation only gradually. In 1970 she expressed herself deeply disappointed that Helen had not been able to have an identical experience of Oxford to her own in the 1930s and was slow to appreciate the extent to which the world had changed, or the degree to which the university had failed to keep pace with either the speed or the direction of that change.

Our Oxford, as graduate students, was simply not her undergraduate Oxford and no amount of squeezing would fit our experience of it into hers. We did understand, though. Place, the stones of Europe from Oxford to Athens and back, exerted an immense attraction on Shirley; she felt its magnetism in her bones. I was to discover that her home city of Wellington was just as powerful a draw on her affections and loyalties. After her death Helen made a donation in her name to the appeal for restoration of the St Hugh's College library, perhaps Shirley's favourite room in all the world, though the Law Society library in Wellington would run it a close second.

She was well known, and rightly so, as a doughty fighter for women's rights and for female equality of opportunity across the whole of society. She had many women friends. She had, in Helen Smith, her brother's wife, one woman intimate. And she had, in Helen Edwards, for many years her secretary and personal assistant, a supporter and helper whose loyalty and honesty she deeply admired, not to say depended on. But what Shirley liked above all was the company of men. She had, through hard work, neglected her social life over the 25 years up to Bill's death and needed somehow to make a new start.

Brian Easton, who had been a colleague of mine at Canterbury University, and whom I thought of as the people's economist, turned a longstanding acquaintance with Shirley into a true friendship that lasted to the end

The library of St Hugh's College, Oxford. Much
restored and modernised since Shirley's day, but
still with the same atmosphere that enchanted her.

of her life, especially in the final sad years, when he was a faithful visitor to her in hospital. Shirley also formed a particular fondness for a friend of ours called Jack Hill. Though barely older than me, he had been one of my lecturers at Keele and then a colleague at Essex, where he stayed for the rest of his university career. Jack read English, BA and BPhil., at St John's College, Oxford, where he had been one of the last pupils of English scholar and Rainer Maria Rilke translator J. B. Leishman and had taken over his tutorials when he died in the Alps in 1963. Jack was a Renaissance literature specialist, an expert on most things from the fourteenth to the seventeenth centuries in France, Italy and Spain, a great friend of Michael Podro, the art historian, with whom he took parties of MA candidates in the history of art on tours to Italy. He took Shirley punting on the Cherwell and regaled her with his conversation.

It would be wrong to call this sparkling, because the term implies a transitory glitter that was never Jack's sort of talk. He was a brilliant raconteur, rich in anecdote, scholarship freed of pedantry, experience turned lightly on a roasting spit of laughter. Shirley adored it. Jack came several times to visit us in New Zealand, making all of us happy, Shirley especially so. And she never missed an opportunity to see him in England. When he sent her one of his volumes of poetry, *Passport to Walk*, he wrote above his signature on the inside fly: 'Punting offers easy memories (but bad rhymes). Con amore.'

Shirley developed a similar attachment to our friends John Ridge and his wife, Irene, again contemporaries not of hers, but of ours, at Oxford. She hugely enjoyed visiting their home above the Ribble Valley in Lancashire, looking out across the fields to the distant walls and towers of Stonyhurst College, where Gerard Manley Hopkins had taught, autumn mists lying in the valley, sunlight glinting off the windows on a summer's dawn, clouds and rain sweeping down from Longridge Fell on a chilly spring afternoon. John and Irene (she is a botanist) had planted a lot of trees, and together they took Shirley for walks, plied her with casseroles and red wine and helped her to learn (John had been an early convert) how to use her first computer, which Helen bought for her.

These people brought her immense satisfaction in life, opening new worlds that her concentrated focus on the law in New Zealand had denied her. All these men made her a bit more adaptable, and they certainly added to her enjoyment of life. When flying to England in 1970, heading for that houseboat in Oxford, she found herself, as she left Los Angeles, sitting among the England football team travelling home from the World Cup in Mexico, where they had just been eliminated by West Germany. Shirley knew nothing of football, rugby was her game, and she must have been one of the few people in the world then who really wouldn't recognise Bobby Charlton or Gordon Banks, Geoff Hurst or Bobby Moore. But she loved the company of young men, gladly agreed to have a drink with Peter Osgood, then another with Jackie Charlton. By the time they arrived at Heathrow, and encountered an astonished Helen who knew exactly who they all were as they said goodbye, Shirley was bosom pals with half the team and spoke glowingly of them. 'Delightful company. Such gentlemen.'

In a quite different register she developed a great fondness for Bill's father, Ebenezer, a man rather excoriated by some in the family for his drinking and his occasional rages, moods that she interpreted as intimations of frustration. In the final years of his life, Bill's mother, Ellen, a strong woman of great spirit and determination, kept her husband almost as a prisoner, confined to his room in the

Wellington suburb of Mornington, a seclusion breached only by occasional visits to the garden. Shirley used to visit him, enjoyed his conversation (as he did hers), was genuinely sorry for him and maintained her concern by continuing to visit him in the psychiatric hospital in Porirua where he spent his last months.

The pleasure she took in diverse, especially male company, real as it was, didn't always translate into self-awareness. Late in life, Helen went with her to a Law Society function in Wellington. As soon as they entered the room a small crowd of senior male jurists — barristers and judges — gathered around her to talk of their mutual experiences of the past, the role Shirley had played in them and their great admiration for her. They towered over her physically, of course, accentuating the frailty of her diminutive height. She was astounded by what they said, by the attention they were paying her, by the obvious sincerity with which it was all expressed. She had no idea that she was remembered at all, let alone in this way. They had particularly vibrant recollections of her teaching them Roman law — a subject deleted from the law degree rubric during her tenure as a lecturer. They all had the strongest memories of it, of its utility to them in later life and practice, and of her vibrant talent as a teacher.

Of course the great majority of her students then, in the late 1950s, had been male. The memories expressed on this occasion were especially strong among those who were the last to have taken the course, when Shirley had ended the year by throwing a toga party. But it was her presence in court that most of them recalled. Shirley, for all her apparent social radicalism, was a great conservative in the law. She loved the common law for its dependence on precedent; she loved the law library as a place to do research, to follow the route of past judgements back through one case to another, examining closely the judicial language employed, seeking the vital difference or similarity between them.

She felt at home in court procedure — gown and wig, 'may it please the court', 'my learned friend', 'your honour' — and she was explicit in telling her clients how they were to behave in the courtroom. She believed in the mystique of the court, saw that its very apartness sustained its independence and thus its impartiality. And what her admirers remembered above all else was that, alongside her great respect for the law and its institutions, went a strong-minded determination to ensure that her clients, whoever they were, benefited from that equality before the law to which she firmly believed they were entitled.

It was this sense of equality that dominated her understanding of feminism. She had no truck with the radical cutting-up-men mobsters. The point was to achieve equality and to ensure that men could enjoy it too. She detested discrimination. After careful scrutiny of the evidence, she was partisan for both Bertolt Brecht and Auguste Rodin against their feminist detractors, and a fierce defender of Ted Hughes from the calumnies of judgemental ignorance. (None of these three gentlemen was, of course, aware of her support.) And woe betide anyone, man or woman, who tried to put her in a box of gender disadvantage. Her determination to ensure that women were included in Wellington Law Society dinners, from which they had been long excluded — a campaign that was ultimately successful, and is now, rightly, a matter almost of legend in legal circles — was waged not really for her own benefit, but for the entire profession. The dinners, as dinners, did not interest her much.

She had extremely good relations with the magistrates of her day (now District Court judges) and respected their honesty and integrity, which she shared. But she was not always able to extend this respect to the police. She was only too aware, in the 1960s and 1970s, of their propensity to commit perjury in court and, as a result, kept a very high opinion of those she knew through observation and experience to be honest, truthful and reliable. There was a mental rogues' gallery certainly, but alongside it she also kept an honours board. As with the law itself, she was interested in the evidence and impartial in judgement. It was this strong understanding of the human element within the constraints of legal procedure that led her, from time to time, to take a close interest in cases that were not hers specifically, but which she felt expressed some more general concern.

So it was with Arthur Allan Thomas, a man convicted of murder on the strength of evidence, as was subsequently shown, that had been planted by the senior investigating detective. Shirley developed a strong friendship with the journalist Pat Booth, who had set his mind to unearthing the reprehensible details of this murky affair, and committed herself to long days of legwork in the search for the truth, including many hours of research in the law library as well as visits to the remote farms that were locations in the crime and its aftermath. Her delight when Thomas, after many years in prison, was eventually cleared of the murders and awarded substantial compensation, was great. She saw it as vindication of her understanding of how a legal system should function: able to correct its errors so as to ensure justice.

She also, I think, felt this search for truth justified in that the effort brought her — and us eventually — another unexpected friendship. Pat Booth's second wife, Valerie, had two children, Victoria and James, whom their mother and stepfather sometimes seemed to find exasperating. Shirley, her own grandchildren having been taken away to live in Paris, offered to have them to stay. Victoria, 12 or 13 years old at the time, quickly adopted Shirley as a friend and confidante. A strong mutual bond developed and on several occasions Victoria came down from Auckland to stay during her school holidays. Shirley took her to films and plays, talked to her about her own past, her life at Oxford and in New York, her understanding of politics and the law and all the books that she read and loved.

In responding to all of this, Victoria got the free run of the house bookshelves. She is now, as Victoria Carter, a successful Auckland businesswoman with strong progressive opinions and leadership skills. Shirley observed the early stages of her remarkable career with great pleasure. Victoria, for her part, never forgot the loving kindness she received from Shirley, wrote to her for the rest of her life, visited whenever she was able and has, much to our benefit, retained us as family friends.

Victoria's experience is indicative. It is a rare generosity on the part of a busy professional woman that she would take time away from a myriad of daily concerns to give devoted friendship to the schoolgirl daughter of friends. Shirley was widely known, and much admired in some circles, as a radical critic and partisan social reformer, but her instincts were largely conservative. A young person needed help and guidance to become a self-sufficient, creative and useful member of society. Shirley saw it as her duty to help. She never flinched or turned away. Any failure, as she might see it in this domain, grieved her greatly.

This glimpse of her generosity gives us an insight into much of Shirley's success in the law. Observers saw, in her occasional defence of Mongrel Mob and Black Power gang members, a crusader for their innocence; the idea that they were misunderstood outcasts from society; that they were not a threat, but an illustration of social inequality and unfairness. In conversation Shirley did sometimes refer to them as 'my boys' but she was no dupe. Their occasional, as it was in those days, serious offending was abhorrent to her and she would tell them so. If one or more of them really had committed the crime with which they were charged, she told them to plead guilty. If not, then she would defend them with every legal device available to her.

What did perhaps set her aside from so many others in the legal system of the 1960s and 1970s was her understanding of the circumstances in which many of them had grown up, and of how the gang environment worked as the first and only safe haven they had ever had. Her pleas in mitigation after conviction and before sentencing were special in this regard.

The underlying social origins of criminal behaviour were never far from her mind. If an instance arose in which she thought she might be able to divert its course, she would take it. Not long before she died, Helen and I found among her papers a sequence of Christmas cards from somebody in Upper Hutt: short messages of gratitude and best wishes. We tracked down the sender and went to visit. He told us how, years before, as a very young man, he had got into trouble with a group of mates, tearaways and delinquents always out looking for trouble after dark. The police had given them the trouble they sought and he had ended up in court charged with a fairly serious crime. Shirley defended him and achieved an outcome that avoided a prison sentence.

This was, like so much of her work, a legal aid case, but even when it was finished she didn't stop there. She kept in touch with the young man, talked to him about the kind of future he was risking, helped him to look for employment and showed him how to manage his life and his opportunities. He never offended again. Every year he wrote to Shirley to reassure her that he was 'going straight' and to thank her for her help without which, he said, he would never have survived. He and his aged mother came to Shirley's funeral, much attended by the great and good of the legal world, sat in a pew right at the back and then slipped away after exchanging a few words with Helen. They may have preferred to leave unnoticed, but we greatly valued their presence, and I like to think Shirley would have valued it at least as much, if not more, as that of most of the others who were there.

I often wondered, over the years, about the source of this concern for the welfare of others, both at the personal and the society-wide level. Shirley could be an intensely serious person; from her earliest teenage years she seems to have performed the tasks she was set with considerable determination. Much of this must surely have come from the Scottish Presbyterian heritage that ran through her father's family, which included significant Presbyterian ministers with free-thinking inclinations. She regarded one ancestor, minister at St Andrew's on The Terrace in Wellington, who had been charged by the Presbyterian Church with heresy, as a hero.

Her own father, Sir David, lost his faith when his young wife, Eva Cumming, died during unnecessary and poorly conducted abdominal surgery when Shirley was only three months old. In the wake of this personal tragedy, he nevertheless retained a turn-of-the-century Presbyterian moral view of the world, free in thought but severe in judgement of wrongdoing. He had, as he once told me, scant enthusiasm for people who were fierce in their demands for their rights, but had little taste for performing their duty.

The dominant injunction was to tell the truth. For Shirley the truth always had a capital T. Behind this injunction stood the figure of her father, whose approval she needed all her life. And beside him the enigma of her lost mother. The absence of Eva, her beauty and serenity, her talents in literature and music, her skill in sport — most particularly tennis: Shirley inherited the cups she won — was a burden to Sir David that I doubt he ever really wanted to put down. Her beauty, the great mound of her lovely auburn hair, the smoothness of her skin, the elegant curve of her neck, they all survive in the few photographs that Shirley treasured and that must surely have worked on her imagination. How different her life would have been if only Eva, like other mothers, had been there for her daughter. If only, if only . . .

Learning of this past, a slow process of accretion in a life that was often focused elsewhere, eventually helped me to stop seeing Shirley as the colonial equivalent of the English privileged public school poseurs of whom I was profoundly suspicious. She was never simply an expression of a class. She was in a class of her own. And a good part of its definition lay in the necessity of her independence. Having no mother she was forced into an independence that became a hallmark, a stamp of identity on the otherwise concealed surface of her character. Bad eyesight, and poor medical advice about it, meant she was kept away from school as a little girl. Poor relations with her stepmother, coupled with a rebellious spirit, led to her being sent, as a young teenager, to a private boarding school where she was desperately miserable and had to fend for herself, learning to be self-sufficient.

When she was only 18, she set off alone on the long sea voyage to England to take up her place at St Hugh's. True, her father paid, she had a decent allowance and when she turned 21 she came into a small trust inheritance from her mother's will, but these were still big steps for a young woman to take then. It was an age away from us now, when to most people she was still a girl, a minor, in need of the university's assumption of a role in loco parentis.

Her tough, individual spirit was born out of these experiences. Coupled with a commitment to the truth as she saw and understood it to be, and her stubborn refusal to be cowed, it became a formidable source of strength. It lay behind her determination to retain her own name when she married. No Mrs Sutch for her. It must have been the same spirit that enabled her to reject the advice, not to say wishes, of both her father and her husband that she not study to become a lawyer. An unbecoming career, in her father's view; an unnecessary neglect of other concerns (what must he have had in mind?) in her husband's.

II

The need for her own independent life stood her in good stead, but its concomitant ferocity and stubbornness could lead to trouble. So it was with the Communist Party of Britain in the 1930s. Shirley spent a deal of time assessing the state of world affairs, something Oxford encouraged then, as it still does. Today people tend to know something, however little, about the horrors of Stalinism and not much about the life and politics of the 1930s. At the time, the reverse was the case. More or less everyone knew much, often by personal experience, about contemporary horrors, but little about the nature of Stalinism. The temptation for the intellectual young to seize on the latter as a cure for the ills of the former was large. It was underscored by the scandal of the Spanish Civil War, by the rise of Oswald Mosley's English fascists, the murderous intimidation tactics of Mussolini's squadristi, the Italian invasion of Abyssinia, the totalitarianism, bellicosity and duplicity of Nazi Germany, and the role of newspapers like the *Daily Mail* in supporting it.

The divisions in society grew wider and deeper almost by the day. If you were to try to write the life of Shirley Smith, you would need to study these matters, to attempt to put yourself in the position of a young person reading the newspapers, seeing the hunger and unemployment on the streets, endeavouring to understand the possibly misguided but genuine decency of the Peace Pledge Union, wishing and hoping for a democratic victory in Spain despite the failure of the European democracies to go to the aid of the Republican cause. Shirley never concealed her steady move towards what is always known (wrongly in my understanding, but that's the academic in me still talking) as the left.

Eventually, like so many others, she joined the Communist Party in 1937. The evidence suggests that, at the beginning, she enjoyed the excitement of the clandestine association she had joined; its demand for obedience. Later, she stopped concealing the commitment she had made then, so that over the years it became a kind of badge people attached to her, as if it defined her whole being. But nothing can convince me of the truth of this. Many years afterwards she talked about it because people kept asking her about it, but I don't believe that it was truly central to her life, perhaps not even back in the late 1930s. Her loyalties lay elsewhere.

What *was* central to her life were the far larger private concerns of her work, her family and her friendships. You don't get a good degree in classics and philosophy at Oxford without a lot of hard work. When she arrived at St Hugh's in October 1935, Shirley's Ancient Greek was the focus of long hours of study in order to catch up with her contemporaries. One of these, Phoebe Llewellyn Smith, was a brilliant classics scholar who must have helped Shirley a lot. Phoebe took a first in Mods and Greats, but she was also a painter and illustrator of note — she had a career, after Oxford, as a book designer and illustrator — as well as a musician and occasional composer.

Shirley was both a friend and a deep admirer of Phoebe.

The main entrance to St Hugh's College, Oxford,
as it was in the 1930s.

She considered her an example of what Oxford stood for as a university, a place of excellence, and she was extremely upset when Phoebe died in what she understood to be a stupid boating accident in the early 1950s. However tough you may be, a death of this sort cannot but lower your morale. Among Shirley's possessions, when eventually she could no longer manage the Todman Street house, we found two paintings by Phoebe. We had them framed and hung them on Shirley's walls at her rest home, where they brought her the solace of good reminiscence.

A parallel tale in a minor key. When the home on Brooklyn hill was badly damaged by water during one of Shirley's overseas absences, many books were ruined beyond repair, among them her battered copy of Lewis and Short's *A Latin Dictionary*. The University of Canterbury Library generously agreed to my request for one of the several copies they had and were having to dispose of. It was similarly battered. The librarian who handed it to me, knowing its destination, said she couldn't imagine a better home. Shirley, on receiving it, found it difficult to choose between weeping and leaping for joy.

At Oxford, if her Ancient Greek needed a little improvement, her philosophy needed to be kick-started. She tore into the subject, especially in its Greek and Latin exemplars and their modern interpreters, even when her progress was impeded by health problems. Shirley developed tuberculosis of some glands in her neck, underwent some initial surgery and then, when the problem returned, went for cure and convalescence to the mountain spa town of Leysin in Switzerland, where Albert Camus was later to go. In her comfortable hospital isolation from the college, her companions and all the library resources of Oxford, she studied on her own, in correspondence with her tutor but otherwise without guidance. Is there a harder way to study philosophy? I very much doubt it. After Easter of 1939 she returned to Oxford for a few weeks to sit finals and was rewarded with a second class degree. They were not further divided in those days, but her tutors were assured that she came close to the top of the class. She always felt unfulfilled by not having a first. I always felt rather astonished that she did so well.

If Shirley was robbed of part of her Oxford experience by illness, she was rewarded in other parts by her eager exploitation of the opportunities that it brought. She participated in one long summer cruise to the historic sights and sites of Greece, the foundation of a deep affection that she never lost. She profited, too, from the friendship of various men whom she met and by the entrée to various quite grand houses that membership of St Hugh's brought with it. She had her first affairs of the heart, though the extent of her sexual experience would be hard to judge today. Shirley retained, long into the second half of the twentieth century, some aspects of Victorian language that, written down in letters, could mislead the unwary. 'Making love', for instance, may well have meant the tentative language and behaviour of polite seduction and not sexual congress. It can be too easy to plaster onto the past assumptions born of more recent presumption.

In the many letters I received from Shirley I always had to search hard for what she was really saying, while the biographer in me was ever conscious of the problems that letters pose. In the right hands they are among the best documentary evidence a biographer can have and there have been fine exponents of the use of them as expository material.[1] But letters can also be a minefield. For a start there is the problem, perhaps not much understood outside the world of biography, of ownership. Shirley's letters, as objects, belong to me, because they have come as a gift, so I am free to dispose of them as I wish. After my death these letters will form part of my estate, like my other goods and chattels, and may be disposed of by my executors. Once, not too long ago, it was considered polite to return letters to their senders after the recipient had died. I did just this with a bundle of correspondence that my father had received down the years from an architect colleague in Edinburgh whom he had particularly admired and whose own family had also become friends of mine. It is regrettable that this practice had begun to diminish even before the decline of letter writing brought on by email.

Ownership of a letter differs, however, from the ownership of its contents, the copyright to which remains the property of the writer and does not pass to the recipient. To quote verbatim from correspondence, biographers must seek permission from the writer of the letter or his or her estate. And it is often over the use of correspondence that projected biographies, especially but not solely of public figures, can come to grief. The owners of copyright can prove difficult, if not hostile, adversaries.

But the biggest problem, especially with letters dating from another century, lies in the meaning of the words and the context of the life of the writer and the recipient. For instance, does anyone know of adolescents or young adults who *ever* wrote truthfully about their lives to their parents? At the very least, it is what is left out that would tell the biographer most. As Aldous Huxley said, '[W]hat is left undone is often as significant in a biography as what is done . . .'[2] And generally, what is selected to be told in this sort of correspondence is a carefully arranged account of what might best meet expectations. A little self-reflection about this (and I have done a lot of it in recent years) yields much.

Then there is the problem of correspondence between lovers. Does anyone know of a lover who wrote to the object of his or her affections without seeking to create some particular effect? There is an old saw that authors generally write their novels for close friends and their correspondence for the general reader. Tchaikovsky endorsed this about composers with a comment that every letter he wrote was a performance. The biographer's task is not so much to accept the document as evidence of what is really happening, so much as to try to tease out the meaning of the performance. The analysis of syntax and the use of language are crucial parts of this enterprise. The biographer is really asking of the letter, to whom was this written? Why was it written, and at this particular time? Why was it composed in this way? And what is missing from it, suppressed into silence?

The other problem I find in Shirley's correspondence is the danger of imprisonment. It is easy to become trapped in its form and language when what is on the page is so partial about experience and in many ways so empty of it. People's ability to write well about their experiences is frequently poor, so that even if someone is seeking to explain an event, the actual description may be woefully inadequate, if not misleading. Shirley's correspondence is an awful warning in this regard. She wrote thousands of letters, many of which have survived, but what they represent now is not so much the ground plan of her life, as evidence of the existence of things in her life which she found hard to confront and from which, psychologically, she was eager to escape. This was displacement activity; she seemed to write the most letters when she was hardest pressed.

She certainly wrote an immense number during periods when domestic circumstances really required her attention, but she felt unable to give it and shied away. In 1990, for instance, when so many aspects of her life were deeply distressing to her, she wrote to us without much reference to them. I doubt that this was to protect us. She was seeking shelter for herself, but it was a strange way to do it. It was generally a pleasure to get a letter from Shirley, but you always wondered what its existence concealed from you, hidden in the byways and cul-de-sacs in which her correspondence abounds.

Sir Geoffrey Cox wrote to me, years ago, commenting on the use of letters, private journals and diary jottings in biography: 'abundant material' should be used in 'judiciously brief quantities . . . The temptation to draw on it more widely' would only clog up the enterprise.[3] This could easily happen to an account of Shirley's life, so full of vitality, movement and energy. The big things lie in her embrace of opportunity, which runs alongside, and not through, her correspondence.

There is some evidence of this in Shirley's commitment to the deep essence of communist persuasion — throwing in your own lot with that of the proletariat, however conceived. It is hard to believe that this fitted into her status in the world. Long afterwards she related two incidents to me that shone a brilliant light into this corner of her life, as well as capturing her sense of wondering self-recrimination about the young woman she had then been. She went to a meeting and dance of the Oxford University Labour Party, where she danced with a working-class boy, as she called him. Towards the end of the evening he asked if he could see her again, take her out. She was dumbfounded. How dare he? What on earth made him think he could possibly have anything in common with her? She had to say no, of course not. It was very embarrassing. I saw it instantly as a moment out of *Jude the Obscure*, 40 years on.

What was I thinking? she said. How could I have behaved like that? And she said it again over an incident at a grand country house weekend, at which she was a guest with her father and stepmother, who had come to Oxford to visit her. She dressed for dinner — this is the 1930s, remember: when Bill accompanied Prime Minister Walter Nash to the Imperial Conference in London he took with him morning dress, including a top hat — and left her stockings and underwear on the floor to be picked up and taken away for laundering. She thought, the chamber maid can do that: it's her job. How could I? Why did I behave like that?

In the deep crevasses of these recollections I detected Shirley re-examining her commitment to communism as an intellectual choice she now understood to be unrelated to her social upbringing, but each a form of hypocrisy, and each feeding off the other to leave her embarrassed and ashamed about both.

In old age, just as in the 1930s, this fiercely independent spirit remained stubbornly committed to the truth and still fighting for it in her own mind. It doesn't do much to answer the question, so often asked about 1930s communism: Why were those committed to the cause unable to see the Soviet Union for what it was? It's a question for psychologists really. Many felt compelled to make a choice and, once made, it stuck for as long as they were prepared to defend it against the evidence. Shirley's commitment to the truth, as she deemed it to be, would require a very great deal of evidence to shift it.

During one phase in my long search for understanding I thought of her as a Janus figure, the two faces indicative of a divided mind: closed on one side, particularly about politics, and also about me for a while; wide open on the other: the law, classics, art galleries, museums, novels and poetry, biography and letters, family, travel, theatre, cinema and parties.

You have to add all of this confusion to the stones of Oxford, to get a real sense of the lifelong importance of the place to her. It wasn't that everything was clear and obvious. It mattered precisely because it *was* muddled and uncertain, filled with experience, unorganised, without linear progression. Joining the Communist Party was part of the confusion generated by the search for order. She defended it later in life because she believed it to have been necessary at the time. But she regretted it too, not because it had damaged her reputation — she couldn't have given a damn about that — but because it had been intellectually wrong. She had misled herself and then been immoveable about it. The fault was hers.

Nevertheless, Oxford was her halcyon age, or at least one in which she had been supremely happy, if not entirely at peace. She treasured it for what it was then and for the memories of it that she carried always. She realised, well before the end of her life, that her instinctive wish for Helen to have the same experiences had contributed to the hurtful split over our marriage. Helen and I had met just two weeks after we each arrived in Oxford from our very different directions. We were graduate students in a university which, in those days, was ideally suited to undergraduates. St Hugh's seemed a petty, stifling sort of institution to Helen, who resented being treated like a schoolgirl, found college rules insufferable (they have all been changed long since) and, apart from some of her tutors and a few friends, found Oxford as a whole intolerably stuffy and class-ridden.

Within a year she and I had become inseparable. To us,

Oxford was more a place to be endured after our separate fulfilling experiences of the University of Michigan and Victoria University of Wellington. This wasn't the Oxford experience that Shirley had enjoyed and which she wanted Helen to have, and I think she regarded me as partly — at first perhaps wholly — to blame. People need their independence certainly, but they also need to find their own way to it, and our way was not, and could not be, Shirley's. Her later regret over her failure to understand this was deep.

That depth is perhaps best illustrated by two incidents seven years apart. It was early October 1971. Helen and I had gone to see Shirley in her office on The Terrace, then a very different street from what it was soon to become. We were to discuss our wedding, four weeks away. Shirley was at her most determined and unbending. She sat like a stone figure behind her desk. We explained the arrangements that we had made, the registry office, the time of day, the simplicity of ceremony. We would like there to be a celebration afterwards. Shirley said we must know how she and Bill felt about the marriage. We had to know the truth. They were opposed. They would come to the registry office, but would not provide a reception, though we might invite people to afternoon tea if we wished. Her manner was so stern and inflexible that I thought of ships' captains, arbitrary judgement at sea, powerlessness. We went out onto a cold pavement and Helen wept in my arms.

It was the night of 10 and 11 January 1978. I had just come home from St Helen's Hospital, where Helen had given birth to our second child. It had been, let us understate it, a busy day. We had been up at the crack of a summer's dawn: our then only child, Piers, was two and enjoyed a 5.30 am start. Helen had been to work at the Treasury as usual. I had been trying to work at home (it was the university vacation) while also managing my parents, who had come for a summer holiday from London. I collected Helen from the office at six o'clock and drove her home, but she went into labour more or less on arrival and we were quickly down to St Helen's. Crispin was born perhaps an hour or so later, still in the preparation room. Quite a bit of panic, some excitable laughter after the unrelieved pain of the birth, much relief, a great deal of exhaustion.

I crawled home late at night, persuaded my parents to go to bed — all was well — and sat for a while, drained but happy, just looking at my feet. Quite suddenly Shirley was knocking tentatively at the back door; she came in carrying a bottle of champagne, which she put on the table. 'You don't have to drink it straight away, but . . .'

'No, no, Shirley, sit down. I'll find the glasses.'

We talked for a couple of hours. Most of what we said is lost to me now, but the great burden of it was hers and the underlying theme: 'If only, if only . . .' How much she regretted, the things that she had thought and said, the failure to understand, all the wrong impulses and suspicions. She was sorry. She was horrified at what she had been. I remember saying not very much, but then Shirley often did a lot of the talking. I was, I hope, too happy about my children and my wife to be uncharitably churlish. Was forgiveness required? I'm not sure she was asking for it. She was, in her genuinely inimitable manner, stating the truth about herself as she now saw it. She had been wrong. 'How could I, how could I?'

I remember the champagne, how good it was, the clink of our glasses as we toasted Helen, the baby, his brother, family, the future. All the usual things. It put, as Helen and I came to see, an end to an unhappy period in our lives. But it wasn't then clear to what kind of family future it might lead. I needed time to adjust, but for Shirley, the change was dynamic. The truth, once recognised and admitted, meant rectification. I was wrong, she was saying. I made a terrible mistake. I have caused a lot of harm. I am truly sorry. Things will be different. I promise.

III

And so they were. She went back over these incidents at the end of her life, when I used to visit her at the Malvina Major rest home; still regretting, still wishing things had been different, but I hope cheered by my assurances, quite truthful long since, that they had been. The children helped, naturally. And Shirley was a terrific grandmother, fitting any and every request into her already crowded life, surrendering the occasional weekend to enable us to get away for a night, always available and forgiving.

But there were other, less obvious indicators. We took back control of various of our personal affairs where she had taken a lawyer's interest in what she had considered her daughter's welfare. And her office ceased to be a place of tension and occasional menace. She was now located in the Dunbar Sloane Building near the old law courts and it became a place of happy rendezvous, especially on Friday evenings, when all the late night shopping got done before the weekend closure. At Christmas it was the welcome base for present shopping, with a gin and tonic awaiting each return to base as the gifts accumulated. And on top of all the improved relations there was Taupō, in the pleasures of which we were fully encouraged to share.

In the late 1920s Shirley's father had bought some land on the left bank of the Waikato River, just on the lip of where it flowed from the lake. It was scrubby pumice land then, with a few trees (including a sequoia, which must have been planted at the turn of the century) and a two-room fishing hut with an open fireplace. Shirley started going there in 1928. There was a precursor to the Desert Road but it was subject to sand drifts and there were rivers to cross,[1] while transport beyond Tokaanu was by boat, so they travelled via Napier, taking most of the necessary provisions with them.

There was a fresh-water spring on the property, fish in the river and lake for food and all the pleasures of a camping holiday for Shirley and her little half-brother, Allan. Over the years, fruit trees were planted, an outside bunkroom added, a tennis court laid down, and finally the front of the hut expanded into a dining and living area, with a broad, shady verandah looking down to the river. Shirley fell in love with Taupō. Morning and evening dips in the river — she was a very strong swimmer — the open fires and the fresh trout cooked on them, the summer days of reading and talking, the trips on the lake in her father's boat, the *Nui*.

It is hard to imagine this scene in the Taupō of today: the unsealed pumice roads, the Māori pā a little up the hill behind them, the river completely uncontrolled (no downstream dams and power stations), the township not much more than the pub and general store, the bird and river life. Shirley formed a bond with this place that grew stronger throughout her life and was the source of some of her greatest happiness and deepest misery. It is easy enough to picture the source of the happiness. There was magic in the place, especially as the trees that Sir David planted grew to maturity, the pumice scrub was turned into grass, the fruit trees brought their annual crops of pears and apples, lemons and walnuts.

It was almost the first place that Shirley went to on her return from Europe in 1939. It was the place to which her thoughts constantly turned when troubles loomed. Bill didn't like it all that much — he was a mountains and bush man for preference — but Shirley was always happy to be there, either with Helen beside her, or on her own with a dozen books to read, the river ever ready for her visits throughout the day. She took her gear up to Taupō in an old green tramper's backpack and slept in the bunkroom.

The misery is less well known, a painful backdrop to her life that her sense of propriety led her not so much to keep secret as to obscure from view. A little of that Presbyterian sense of family, perhaps. The difficult truth — there it was again — was that her brother, Allan, while she was away for 10 of the 15 years from 1935, formed an equally deep attachment to the Taupō property and came to think of it as his. By the early 1950s he had a rapidly growing family and a busy doctor's practice and along with his (and our, as it happens) close friends, the Sakers, required possession of the property every year for Christmas and the month of January, a need that Shirley felt unable to challenge.

It meant that her summers, after 1944, never again included the free life of Taupō. When Sir David died in 1982, not long before his ninety-fourth birthday, Allan was astonished and bitter to discover that, contrary to what he had always expected, his father had left the property to him and Shirley jointly. Allan's behaviour over this, among many other aspects of his domestic arrangements, had a distinctly Victorian tarnish to it. Shirley contributed half the money to pay the bills — rates and insurance and so on — and Allan took the decisions on how to run the property without bothering much to consult. There was an obsessional aspect to this which Helen and I, when at our best, found funny, but which was most often simply distressing. In the 1970s and 1980s, for instance, whenever, with permission, we slipped away to Taupō for a weekend, Allan would arrive too, unannounced, generally late and noisily on a Friday night, having driven up from Wellington on his own. Somehow, he just couldn't bear that we were there unsupervised.

If head you can call it, things came to one in 1990, when Allan decided that a new and better house should be built on the property, and went ahead and organised it. This time there was some consultation, but the choosing of the Lockwood home, the location on the site, the dates of building and ultimately the cost were all settled more or less without Shirley's participation, only her formal agreement, which she felt compelled to give: powerless to withhold it, but wounded by it, too. Deeply conservative about domestic matters by then, she never wanted Taupō to be changed in any way.

Shirley kept only an appointments diary, but in 1990 it contained cryptic entries on this and other events. It was a terrible year. She learned of the new house project in mid-February. At the end of July Allan told her he wanted $50,000 from her for it. 'Horrors,' she wrote. A week later the sum had gone up another $15,000. She certainly didn't have this money. By the end of August the proposal was that instead of contributing to the capital cost she should take 'a lesser interest' in the property, an idea that Allan said was his. 'News to me.' By the end of November: 'Taupō again. V. angry.'

Shirley detested her own powerlessness over Taupō, but somehow she couldn't overcome it. Her ownership of the property was reduced from half to a third. It made her feel that she had failed. But there was something about these Smith males, her father and her brother, that she felt unable to confront. They, alone of all the world, could defeat her.

In her father's case it was a defeat by kindness. She did much of which he disapproved, in politics, in the man she married and in keeping her own name, in taking to the law as a career, in not, as he saw it, properly looking after her health when she was at Oxford. But although he would have found these things unforgivable in others, he readily forgave them in Shirley. She was the daughter of the woman he had loved and lost. She was not just the reminder of his Eva, but also the embodiment of her in life. To Shirley, so like her mother in looks and talent, he permitted a largesse of tolerance others could not hope to have, however they might strive to earn it. Shirley responded by seeking his support and wanting his approbation for everything she did, and he readily gave it, often along with much wise advice.

In the case of her brother Allan, Shirley's feelings of powerlessness stemmed from an inability to break the unwritten laws of family propriety. What she knew of him she feared in him, but couldn't confront him because that was not how families should behave. She also knew that, as a boy, Allan may have suffered badly from comparison with her. Unlike his blessed older sister, he had had to earn every ounce of his father's approval. Often enough it had been withheld. It created a resentment that may have been one source of his feelings about Taupō and its place in their lives. Shirley had had everything else in terms of their father's affection; surely he, Allan, was entitled to this.

There are elements of *Middlemarch* and *Buddenbrooks* in all of this, writ small it is true, but with no less disheartening effects on the participants and as often as not leading to similar reflections on the moral components of life. When her father came to visit Shirley in Oxford in 1938 he commissioned a bust of her by the English sculptor Alec Miller. To my knowledge there is no equivalent of Allan. Left behind at school in New Zealand, what would he have made of that, and of his parents' pleasure in the artefact? Such differences in treatment do not go unnoticed in families, either at the time or later in life.

Allan's wife Helen (nee Wilson), whom he met in Dunedin when they were both students at Otago University in the late 1940s, grew up on a farm at Piopio in the King Country. She was the granddaughter of Helen Wilson, a redoubtable woman of exceptional fortitude and integrity,[2] and, like her, was capable of taking in her stride whatever life might throw up. Shirley greatly admired Helen and the two women became close friends and confidantes. They exchanged many intimacies, often in the company of their mutual friend, Gay Saker. All three women had reason to admit in private that they lived in damaged relationships and over the years it became obvious to us that Allan's behaviour, to his wife, to his children and eventually even to one of our own grown-up sons, was reprehensible. There is, we believe, documentary evidence of at least some of this in letters that Helen Smith wrote to Gay Saker, who promised to let my Helen have them after Gay died.

The course of any life is inevitably profoundly influenced by experience in childhood and adolescence, generally and most obviously by parents. How could it be otherwise? In the case of the Smith family, in which one parent exhibited clear signs of bad faith while the other was deeply caring and loving, the emotional turmoil of each child was surely great. I first met Allan and Helen's daughter, Jenny,

Bust of Shirley by Alec Miller (1879–1961), wood, 17 x 15 x 13 cm, 1938. Miller, who had come from a very poor Scottish background to become a leading ecclesiastical carver in England, was a cousin of Shirley's father, Sir David Smith. He emigrated to the United States in 1939. The National Portrait Gallery in London holds his bust of Laurence Housman.

in the early 1970s, when she was a teenager planning to go to university in Auckland to study architecture. She was a young woman of immense joie de vivre and immoderate beauty, adaptable, sociable, outgoing. There seemed to me no limit to what she might accomplish. By the mid-1980s she was trapped in anorexia from which she never recovered and which led her to a drifting half-life and what seemed to me to be the indicators of despair. The self-harm of the disease was evidence of a need to punish someone for what had happened to her. It was just that she picked the wrong person to punish. She died in India at the age of 57.

Much of the regret with which Shirley wrestled late in her life was about Jenny, that she had never tried hard enough to help her niece, had never intervened to take her under her wing and look after her, had never attempted to discover what might have happened to her and to support her in overcoming the trauma. If only, if only . . .

Some people, daring to be duplicitous and manipulative, can nevertheless escape censure by adopting a hail-fellow, well-met style that serves as moral camouflage. Both intentions and actions are obscured by the façade of agreeable bonhomie that amuses even as it dissembles, and is protected by family discretion. The camouflage thus thrown over the surface of family life can obscure the malicious moral transgressions that lead to lasting suffering. Shirley tried to believe that there was some good in everyone, and succeeded most of the time; you just had to know where to look for it. It meant she could be deceived, but once aware of the deception she was quick to remedy her position and only really ready to blame herself for the original mistake.

There was another example of this in the 1980s, though in a much more minor key. She had been reunited at her seventieth birthday party with a former client called

Paul Lanczy, a New Zealander of Hungarian extraction, exuberant, full of the kind of life force that brooked no argument and seemed equipped to overcome any obstacle. In the celebratory atmosphere they incubated a plan to travel together one summer through central Europe, going to his home and birthplace and visiting the cities, galleries and museums of which Shirley had read. Had she not been an early devotee of Patrick Leigh Fermor and the romance of his famous walk across Europe?

The pair of them subsequently hatched this plan in the northern summer of 1987: Austria, Czechoslovakia (as it then was), Hungary, Poland and possibly even on into what was still (though only just) East Germany. My memory of what would be is clouded by Shirley's account of what was. By the time the couple reached Prague in the rental car for which they had jointly paid, Shirley was a wet rag. Paul was an impossible travelling companion: determined to have his own way in every detail (there were no stops for the sights or the museums), quick to anger, often dangerous behind the wheel but refusing to let her drive, an obstinate bully in every aspect of the journey.

In Prague Shirley became deeply afraid. She went to her room after dinner and packed her case. At dawn she got up, walked in fear from the hotel to the railway station without speaking to a soul and bought a ticket back to the West. It took her weeks of rest in the company of friends in Britain to recover. Even so, she blamed herself. If only she had paid more attention from the start she would have realised the danger and never agreed to go. It was my mistake. People are who they are and I should have known.

Her 33-year relationship with Bill was, naturally, of a completely different order. She had met him when she was ready to marry. She was 25 in 1941, well past the age then thought proper for marriage, and she wanted children. Bill was very handsome and talented. They shared a view of politics and the world. That he had come out of the working class by his own efforts appealed to her; that she was from the kind of establishment family that might bring security and stability appealed to him. It was love and mutual admiration, with probably, too, the frisson of daring that came from his adultery, far more socially punishable then than it appears to be now. Shirley believed, and said as much to me, that Bill had never loved Morva, whom she knew and had frequently seen in Bill's company, and had married her only to protect her reputation in the wake of the Tararua tramping incident. He was keen to free himself from her and married Shirley as soon as his divorce came through.

Shirley must have known before she married him that Bill could be difficult. She told me how he didn't want anyone to come to their wedding, just a couple of friends to act as witnesses. I rather sympathised with him in this. I hadn't really wanted anyone at my own wedding either and had suggested to Helen that we do it in a registry office one Thursday afternoon when no one would be looking. In the event we were foiled by my mother, who came out from London for the occasion.

Families can be funny about weddings. There is the sense that their presence is an entitlement, that witness must be borne. In Bill and Shirley's case it was Shirley's Cumming relatives who found out about the occasion because Shirley couldn't bear not to let her grandmother know. The bush telegraph brought them out in numbers, ready to bear witness and to celebrate. In our case I was content to let things go ahead as they would. There had been enough trouble and I wasn't eager for more. On our wedding night my mother slept in our bed in our rented flat in Wai-te-ata Road and Helen and I slept on the floor at a colleague's house. Bill, by then 35, was rather less flexible at his own wedding to Shirley, or perhaps accommodating is the better word. He was appalled when the relatives turned up, went into a sulk, couldn't be appeased for a couple of days. Shirley's disappointment was great.

There were to be other disappointments along the way. Bill was often absent, first when called up for army service, then in Sydney for UNRRA, to which posting she followed him, then in Southeast Asia also on UNRRA business, when he contracted dysentery and malaria and was hospitalised in Wellington in 1945 before being sent to London on European UNRRA work in 1946. Shirley gave birth to Helen in Sydney in mid-November 1945. It was a terrible experience, the labour lasting into a third day, hospital staff unsympathetic, Bill beside himself with anxiety, the baby eventually pulled into the world by forceps, covered in blood. Bill made up his mind that there would be no more children: the danger and the pain were too great. Shirley told me that she agreed with him, but Helen feels that it was, rather, acquiescence. But then people's views about this sort of thing change as the recollection of distress recedes.

The memories of these things that Shirley set down in her old age are among the most difficult parts of her writing to interpret. She wasn't writing them for publication, of course, but for her immediate family, and perhaps with two things in mind. One was that we should know and understand. The other was that the pieces should have the feel of some sort of legal document, and in doing so distract attention from other subjects. An affidavit perhaps. The truth. She wouldn't varnish events.

There would be no sentimentalising. There wouldn't even be much context: where we were, what it was like, what we read and ate together, what we visited, what we saw. The syntax would convey bare facts as she saw them. One obvious consequence of this was that she, as far as I know, never wrote anything about her half-brother, his family, what had happened to them, particularly her niece, Jenny.

Something every good biographer learns is to listen to the silences. When I was researching the life of Dan Davin I quickly came to understand that where there were gaps in his diary, or when a notebook of diary entries had been lost, it was an indicator that he had started some new liaison. By the time Shirley wrote her reminiscences in the late 1990s she was a troubled soul, certainly, but the troubles really attached to her awareness of her declining cognitive powers and her inability to write anything about Jenny and the causes of her terrible circumstances. Her sense of grief and regret about this must have been immense, but she couldn't shift it by writing the truth as she understood it to be, not even for her own daughter.

What she did write might best be seen as avoidance, or even as substitute documentation; something critical to obscure, if not make invisible, the real hurt with which she felt compelled to live in silence. The result is, in the case of what she wrote about Bill, an invitation to see him as almost a cartoon character, a cut-out. Beyond those of us who knew him well the prose could serve as an invitation to invent. If you showed it to someone of the 'Bill-as-weasel' persuasion they would find in it the kind of ammunition they preferred. It could be made to fit their case. At the end of her life, they might say, she had seen him for what he was. What they also might be saying, however, is that she was taken for a fool. But this was not true of Shirley, who was perspicacious, lively minded, often adept at detecting merit.

What is so interesting is the extent of the silences within the piece itself. It has nothing to say about their love affair, the pillow talk of their hopes and ambitions, the pride they took in their work, in their daughter, in their careers. There is no real account of where and when they met, of the excitement that she felt, of how she took him as a lover and wished to be married to him and him alone, when so many other perhaps equally attractive men had wanted her. It's almost an exercise in concealment. Nothing about Mary Redmer/Josephson. Nothing about suspicions of other lovers. Nothing about the conversations that she had with her sister-in-law, Helen Smith, or about her nephews and niece, for all of whom she cared deeply.

A lot of what we profess to know is derived from what we are told. But what people tell us is not always true, except in the sense that it conveys some truth about the person doing the telling. What is it he or she is telling me? Why is it being told? And why is it being told like this? In this regard Shirley's late writing, especially about Bill, is enigmatic.

It is silence that often speaks loudest, what is not said that resonates the most. After puzzling over these pieces for 20 years, I have concluded that, whether deliberately or not, the guidance they appear to give about Shirley's life is really a diversion, pointing us away from family problems which she cannot bear to relate.

Our house in Konstancin-Jeziorna, where she penned these pieces, was the home of a diplomat who was then Poland's ambassador to Syria. The property included a little guesthouse in the garden, shaded by trees, with its own living space and bedroom. This was where Shirley stayed and wrote. I remember that summer: beautiful long, hot days; the best raspberries I have ever tasted; the pleasure I was taking in my own writing, which resulted in two novels that Hamish

Hamilton published in London. Shirley came in every day for her meals, most of which I prepared because Helen was working long hours in Warsaw, and we talked a lot across the kitchen table. It was obvious to me then that her mind was not what it had been, and there were occasional incidents in the evenings when her general tolerance might suddenly disappear and she became charged with an uncharacteristic aggression in conversation.

At some point Helen took her mother off with her for a number of days on a business trip to Riga in Latvia, where Shirley explored the churches and towers, the fine city buildings from the times of the Hanseatic League, and the Art Nouveau architecture of a turn-of-the-century quarter where both Sergei Eisenstein and Isaiah Berlin had spent their early years. She and Helen made a weekend trip, escorted by one of Helen's knowledgeable Latvian colleagues, to the small towns and villages scattered across the countryside, to the beauty of which Shirley responded with immense pleasure.

Latvia and Poland had not had much of what economists call development over the preceding 50 or 60 years, though almost all the war damage had been repaired. With the exception of Jewish life, which had been butchered out of existence and the evidence of it smoothed from the sight of all but the most diligent of searchers, this was still, visually, very much the Europe Shirley had known and visited in the 1930s.

Her pleasure in it greatly influenced her thoughts about her own life, not poisoning but repositioning them. The 'If onlys' of her discourse became more frequent, more heartfelt. Landscape, those long summer days, the tranquillity of our lives, returned her to another time, filling her with memories. In general Shirley was not nostalgic about the past. She became rather critical of her own part in it; a criticism that she integrated into her reserve about personal, intimate matters. She told me once that Bill had been a very good lover, but otherwise she volunteered little about her personal life as a young woman, or her fantasy life as an adult. (She was only 58 when Bill died.)

She thought about these things, though. She had read enough Freud to have a handle on his theory of childhood trauma and its link to neurosis. She was deeply interested in her dreams, tried hard to remember and write them down and I'm sure thought hard about their meanings. I came to the view that her late writing was really an act of personal resistance. She felt that she ought to tell us something, but when it came to the task she shied away. Her truth she would keep to herself. What we were left with was not even what British poet Christopher Caudwell called a 'decent skeleton'.[3]

It's a kind of mortal challenge to any would-be biographer, but it does bring into focus Shirley's occasional complaint about neglect. All her life she would say she had been defined as the daughter of Sir David Smith, then the wife of Bill Sutch and eventually the mother of Helen Sutch. These three successful people had somehow, in the public mind, shouldered her out of the way. It was very demeaning.

In the piece about Bill, she is pointing out, by not saying, that yes, I was married to Bill, but he wasn't by any means my whole life. That was my own to live. And I lived it. She particularly resented the idea — widespread, as she thought and feared — that her life had been defined, just as the weasel believers defined Bill's, by the trial and the role in it which she was allotted by public opinion. Faithful wife. Diligent legal researcher on his behalf. Joyous victor at his acquittal. Terrier in his defence from all the malice and spite of the many years that followed. This stuff stuck to her.

But it wasn't then, and it never should have been allowed to become, the definition of her. Apart from selecting his defence counsel, Mike Bungay, Shirley made almost no contribution to Bill's defence. Nor really, let it be said at long last, did Mike Bungay, who very brilliantly performed his role as swaggering courtroom performer and advocate, but otherwise was led by the brilliance of his partner, Ian Greig.[4] During and after the trial, Shirley diligently supported Bill at home and lovingly nursed him through the painful final seven months of life. But she was his wife. It was her role. What else would be expected of any of us? It didn't define who she was as a person.

Other things, apparently trivial, or rather, important but so transient in everyday life as to escape attention, help to fix her in my memory. In Shirley's life there were the pinks. Her beloved grandmother, with whom she lived until she was seven years old, delighted in these little carnations and Shirley grew up loving them, too. She had cuttings taken from her grandmother's pinks and planted them in Wellington. They became the principal focus of her interest in the garden. She then transplanted them from her father's home in Wadestown to her own in Brooklyn.

After Bill died she bought a big wooden planter for them and installed it in the courtyard. The pinks were lovingly weeded and watered, new cuttings taken, the blooms occasionally cut to bring indoors, or as a gift for her sister-in-law. They were of immense importance to her. When, towards the end of her life, she failed to maintain them, and the last of them died, she felt it as a break from her own roots, a breach in what she held dearest. They were both a guide and a link to some of the most important threads in Shirley's life: family and fidelity, continuity and reliability, simple pleasures and self-help, a public world of radical service in the context of a private world of simple conservative values.

Two days after Bill died, when the four of us — Shirley, Helen, I and our 12-day-old baby — were together at the house in the evening, there was an unexpected ring at the door. Helen answered it. On the steps outside were some 30 women from the Cook Islands community, in their traditional dress. They asked very politely if they might come in, as they wished to tell us of their sorrow at Shirley's loss. They came upstairs to the living-room, settled on their knees in a great arc and sang, perhaps for an hour or so. Hymns of sorrow and lament. Hymns of love and sympathy. Hymns of hope and promise. Then they rose and gravely departed.

They were there not for Bill, but for Shirley. She was the one, the woman, the strength. She had looked after them and helped them for many years. They counted her one of their own, a membership which, by extension, Helen and I were privileged to share. She wasn't David's daughter, Bill's wife, Helen's mother: she was wholly her own self. Among our many photographs of Shirley is one taken in Golden Bay in January 1976. It shows her with our four-month-old son, Piers, wrapped in a shawl in her arms, walking on the sandy track beside the bach we had rented. She is singing to him. She had put Bill behind her. Yes, she defended him courageously at any and every new misrepresentation, as she saw it, as the years went by. But she was a woman for the future, really, and in any event she was also doing her lawyerly duty, defending the legal system that she treasured. He had been acquitted, had he not?

Soon, when this holiday in Golden Bay was done, she would return to work and all the battles on behalf of others that awaited her there. And her legal practice was in a dire state. Two of the people she had been employing for the previous few years had, without her realising, been turning her entire office into a pro bono operation. She had to let all her staff go, other than the indomitable Mrs Edwards, and devote herself to representing and billing clients. She worked immensely long hours, completely absorbed in the tasks at hand. Our full reconciliation still lay in the future, but I had to admire her focus.

As further proof, if it were needed: One night in the early 1950s, Shirley was driving on Wellington's Molesworth Street. Suddenly she knocked down a pedestrian, who subsequently died. There was, obviously, an inquest, as a result of which she was exonerated. There had been witnesses. The man had reeled into the road in front of her and there was nothing she could have done. I am vague on the details because I only learned of the event recently: Shirley did not mention it to Helen or me, though it figured, apparently, in her father's manuscript autobiography. Somehow Helen, still a little girl at the time, had been screened from it. It must be terrible to feel that you have caused another's death, even if absolutely no fault attaches to you. With Shirley's intense sense of responsibility, and the need to face the truth, the burden was, I imagine, great. Oh, if only I hadn't been there at that moment; if only the last set of traffic lights had delayed my progress. If only, if only . . . The other thing to note, of course, is the family silence on the event. No one ever referred to it.

Shirley, a classicist, knew Aeschylus' *Oresteia* trilogy, where the Eumenides — known euphemistically as the Kindly Ones, or the Gracious Ones — are the Furies at work in our lives. In 1990, that terrible year, out of the blue, Shirley was served a writ of defamation on behalf of a woman called J. A. Andrews. She wanted half a million dollars. I know none

Eva Cumming, Shirley's mother; the lost
love of Sir David Smith. I can see in her
her granddaughter Helen, and she looks
unquestionably the great-grandmother of
our sons. They could hardly ask for better.

of the details, which apparently arose out of some other long previous case, but it seems to have unnerved Shirley badly. Rather than defend herself, she engaged Sandra Moran as her lawyer, and much of the spring was taken up with preparing her own affidavit and securing those of others.

She was deeply rattled, however, sensing that the case was spurred by some sort of personal animosity. 'Malice makes me sick,' she wrote in her appointments diary on 17 October. A month later her legal colleague Bill Gazley was in touch with advice: 'Don't apologise. Stand up and fight.'[5] She did, and the case was thrown out, but it cost Shirley some tens of thousands of dollars in legal fees, money that she could ill afford to spend.

As if this were not enough, the trauma of the case came on top of a burglary at the Brooklyn house. Shirley was visiting us in Washington, where we had moved at the beginning of September 1989, but had been there for only three weeks when news arrived that thieves had stolen the two Chinese ceramic horses from her living-room at home. They were both beautiful pieces, the larger one T'ang in style (there was much argument whether it was an original or a copy) and the other Han, and certainly original.[6] Shirley had to change her tickets and return home. Somehow, through her contacts in the underworld — Shirley had been involved in criminal law cases for over 30 years in our still very small society — she was able to trace the works. Unable to sell such a rare piece, the thief or thieves had already smashed the T'ang horse into a million pieces. The Han horse, damaged though not irreparably, she was able to get back. She never said how. For the rest of her time in Brooklyn the glass case that Plischke had designed specifically for the T'ang horse stood empty. Shirley perhaps felt it as a reproach, certainly as a hole in her life.

In July of 1990 she took a course in transcendental meditation. Perhaps this signalled a change in her way of life. She had given up her office in town and been working as a lawyer from home for a number of years; now she devoted more time to her friends, her correspondence and her interests. For many years she had, in spring and summer, gone for a late afternoon swim in Oriental Bay. In the late 1970s she would take Piers with her, his first instruction in swimming; she also taught him the rudiments of cricket. She swam well into her eighties.

When the film festival came around she would invite a friend to go with her, particularly to European films — German, French and Italian — where she had enough of the languages to follow without the subtitles. Afterwards she would take herself and the friend — Helen Smith, or Gay Saker (now her near neighbour) or Cecilia Johnson, the widow of the poet Louis Johnson and daughter of her old friend Ormond Wilson[7] — on somewhere to supper, much favouring the cuisine of Lois Daish. During the New Zealand Arts Festival she would take Bill's sister Shirley to the ballet and dance performances, which she loved.

She also turned to her books, her letter writing and to amazingly strenuous travel as, perhaps, displacement activities for the areas of her life she could not bear to face. Part of the difficulty was that she was not very well off. Bill had made Mike Bungay his executor and he, distracted no doubt as much by his murderous caseload as by the quantity of whisky that he drank, did not have the estate wound up until the mid-1980s, 10 years after Bill's death. There was precious little in it for either Shirley or Helen, or anyone else for that matter. The great wealth he was said to have, mainly via SIS-inspired rumour, certainly never came to any of us.

Shirley had never sought wealth through her legal career. A lot of her work was via legal aid. Many other clients never paid. She cared deeply about the matrimonial cases that came to her in ever greater numbers — another connection with Bill Gazley, a fearsome advocate in this field with whom she would discuss cases. What financial security she did have came from her father's estate, which included substantial investments on the stock market. Because Shirley took little or no interest in these, she believed that she had lost little when the Roger Douglas/America's Cup-inspired fools' bubble collapsed in 1987 and the value of her shares retreated to more or less the same level as when she inherited them in 1982.

To add to the income from these she had half of Bill's two small pensions and her own national superannuation. It was hardly wealth. Even so, she gave much away, either to charities or by always buying an artwork or a book at the openings and book launches to which she was invited. To finance her occasional need for capital, she would sell a few parcels of shares, but never the investment in Brierley's that her father had accumulated. She held onto them as an article of faith until they, too, collapsed and disappeared in the late 1990s.

Home and away Shirley read voraciously. She revelled in 1930s detective novels, especially those by Margery Allingham and Dorothy Sayers, and loved the books of Nancy Mitford and Barbara Pym, Margaret Atwood and Janet Frame, Jane Austen, Margaret Drabble and P. G. Wodehouse. She developed a passionate interest in the Bloomsbury Group, buying and reading every volume of Virginia Woolf's diaries and letters, along with the biographies of Gerald Brenan and Ottoline Morrell, Vanessa Bell and the Nicolsons, Dora Carrington and Lytton Strachey, and many others. She had much in common with their high-minded dissent and clarity of bohemian intelligence.

These interests were at one with her lifelong passion for Greece, its history and landscape. At Oxford she had nurtured a particular affection for and interest in Ancient Greek art and pottery, for which she retained an intense aesthetic delight, and I never saw her happier than on a Cretan archaeological site in 1984, where much had to be imagined and the atmosphere took your breath away. The gift from her that I value most is a copy of an ancient amphora from the museum in Heraklion. It is a lovely piece which I would never have thought to buy for myself, but I understood its meaning to Shirley: here is something of what I treasure most in this world, and in which I would like you to share.

Such generosity, such giving of the self, embraced the intense love that she felt for her daughter and her grandsons. This must have included a profound sense of good fortune that her behaviour over our marriage had not led to the loss of Helen's support and affection. She knew, though, that it had greatly adjusted the relationship and that she had been immensely lucky to have retained Helen's love. She may well have feared that she had come close to losing it.

In old age, as the dementia to which she increasingly succumbed took hold, she started to be a bit cranky and could be cantankerous. At our dinner table in Poland — she was well into her eighties and we had, on a recent visit to Wellington, seen with some dismay how badly the house in Brooklyn needed maintenance — Helen tried to discuss with her mother the management of her future years. All of Shirley's indomitable spirit came hurtling to the surface, like a swimmer who had done the first two lengths under water. Not only was she not getting old but, she almost shouted, 'I am never going to die.' She really did say this. The Brooklyn house would be taken in hand; so would the garden. She looked as fierce as she sounded. It was all one with how she would come to the table, first clearing the carefully laid cutlery away from her place, then placing her arms down before her, establishing a presence that spoke of readiness for combat.

Helen, who was deeply concerned about her mother's welfare, courageously persisted, but I, a weakling, thought it best to creep away to my bed. When Shirley was in battle mode it was no contest. In this connection she often talked of two of her uncles on the Cumming side of the family, one of whom had lived to be 102, and the other, Uncle Willy, to be 106. She was in no doubt that she would emulate, if not surpass them. It was pointless to dwell on alternative possibilities: this was audacity in the grand style. Napoleon at Austerlitz. It doesn't always work to your advantage. It can lead to serious trouble.

Often, however, as she surely knew, the trouble was worth it. After she died John Clarke, a friend of mine since the 1970s, wrote to me about Shirley and her life from his home in Melbourne, where he managed the impossible, living the quiet domestic life of a brilliant writer while being a media star: 'questioning the system is good for the system but requires great spirit and resolve, since the beneficiaries of the unimproved system will engage in constant personal attack on all fronts and have everything to lose. And even when they are exposed and defeated, it will be reported as a victory.'

Thinking of this 'spirit and resolve' always returns me to other quite contrasting images of her. Feet up on her office desk at lunchtime, with the paper, a sandwich and then a cigarette. Parsons' Bookshop café for early morning coffee and the day's mail. Her love of dogs, particularly our English labrador, Artemis, whom she enjoyed walking in Washington and Warsaw — though Artemis looked almost as big as

Minoan amphora, clay, circa 1500 BCE. A copy
from the museum in Heraklion, a piece of
something that Shirley treasured most in this
world, and which she wanted me to share.

Shirley. Her laughter at some of the simple absurdities of life, such as Bill's successor at Industries and Commerce being called Moriarty, or at the time of Bill's trial our solicitor-general being Savage and our chief justice Wild. The cold bath with which she started every day. Rugby test matches, which she listened to on the radio. One of her proudest memories was to have sat next to George Nepia, the great Invincibles fullback of 1924–5, on the platform of the Wellington Town Hall for a 'No Maoris No Tour' protest meeting. Her deep love of the many moods and colours of Wellington which, despite Oxford, was the place of her heart and home, her tūrangawaewae. The *Palgrave's Golden Treasury* of English poetry, which had belonged to her mother and which she took with her everywhere. She knew a lot of it by heart.

And her correspondence. Shirley was one of the great letter writers, certainly in volume if not always in style. Everyone got letters, from Nikita Khrushchev and Patrick Leigh Fermor to the nameless drone who sent out *Reader's Digest* 'you are definitely a winner' lottery forms that Shirley's diminishing cognitive powers led her to believe meant financial security late in her life. When, as a result of a stroke in early September of 2005, she lost the use of the right side of her body, her letter writing, and her walking, came to an end. She felt it as a death of sorts. Further disabling neurological events followed, progressively robbing her of almost all her mental powers.

Summing up what was important to her in life, she said to Helen, 'I'm no use now, am I? Not to anyone.'

Her letters convey a very direct sense of her love of life, and of her seriousness about it. Both were tempered by a profound sense not of guilt — with the singular exception of Jenny Smith she didn't, I think, suffer from that — but, progressively, of loss, as though not having seen the truth of things at the time had robbed her sensibility, negated opportunities she might otherwise have taken. She felt this particularly strongly over the disastrous neglect and destruction of the environment in much of central and eastern Europe to which she felt her eyes had been closed by obstinacy; and also in the matter of friendships, so many of which, through constant concentration on her legal work, she had let slip. These losses through neglect had removed the opportunity to be of even greater service to the world than she had been. This was the full and true meaning of 'Oh, if only, if only . . .'

But this lament was not her sole frequent saying and is too rueful to be the last word here. There was another expression, born of her Scottish heritage, and serving as a response to all the calumny and ignorant lies of the merciless world of half-truths, ridicule and envy from which she had suffered, and against which she had stood. She never said it but with its proper air of stubborn defiance:

They say. What say they. Let them say.

Between memoir & biography

A note on lives lived in words

There has been quite a lot of loose speculation in recent years about the role of imagination in all writing about the past — history as well as biography. Much would be gained from repositioning the disputes arising from such speculation on the obligations of historians and biographers, rather than the pleasures or desires of readers, or the creative 'liberty' or 'imaginative understanding' of writers.

Nobody, surely, would ever pretend that 'The Life' of a person on paper can ever be the same as the life itself. How could it possibly be? But the starting point in the effort to bring the two together — which is, after all, what biography seeks — is the recognition that fidelity to the facts of a life as it was lived should serve as the foundation, and that to stray from the existence of these facts — and as accurate a transmission of them as possible — is an act of betrayal that robs the subject of his or her true existence in the world.

By imposing the possibly false or the imaginatively inaccurate, the free interpretation of motivation and purpose in a life that may flow from factual errors, omissions or distortions, the biographer may obscure, even risk eliminating, the complexities of another's life. People do have motivations and purpose in life and, where strongly held, they tend to be true to them. But how to test the strength of someone's purpose? Biographical invention can amount to theft, robbing the subject of his or her own autonomy as a person.

In her 1927 essay, 'The New Biography', Virginia Woolf, in insisting that biography must adhere to the facts of a life, writes about truth as 'something of granite-like solidity'. But that notion has done much harm to all thinking about biography.[1] The problem, as always, is in the splice that cuts between the neutrality of careful research methodology and the rhetorical utility of words like 'truth'. Productive thought and discussion about biography would be much enhanced by agreeing, if only it were possible, to exclude this word from the debate.

Woolf's essay does help to remind us, however, that, as with writing about history, biography begs for the requirements of scholarship ahead of the narrative skills of fiction. And there is no ducking the fact that scholarship really consists less of a set of methods and more of a cluster of injunctions that steer research behaviour away from the pleasures of free interpretation, and towards the much harder, though ultimately far more fertile, ground of self-limiting personal conduct.[2]

Understood in this way, biographical scholarship begins with humility, which provides for an assumption of care and doubt before any piece of evidence. Is this evidence reliable? If it is true, for whom is it true? Everyone? Or just the teller of it? What does it mean? How should it be interpreted?

After humility comes modesty, a proper understanding of one's own limitations. Do I have the training, the skill, the talent to understand and interpret the evidence? It is obvious that you cannot undertake the biography of someone whose first language you do not speak. The same surely applies to a biography of a mathematician. Or a musician. Or a philosopher. Who could possibly have confidence in a life of Fermat, Joachim or Mosca by someone with no knowledge of maths or music or political and social theory? And especially not if it were written, say, by a popular novelist looking for some expanded recognition as a 'life-writer'?[3]

In any intellectual field, mastery of large and constantly expanding literatures demands focus and study. Any individual life can be translated into 'The Life' on paper only with a steady scholarly focus on both the intellectual matter and the lived experience of the biographer's subject.

After modesty comes application. This is a form of knowledge in itself: knowing where to seek evidence; knowing what weight to attach to it; knowing how to test it against sources; knowing, above all perhaps, how to select from that 'blizzard of specific data that is a personal life'.[4] All of this, in turn, adds up to a searching examination of the writer's stamina and independence.[5]

The sum of these requirements is integrity, which is the basis of trust, both the writer's for his or her account of past events and circumstances, and the reader's. The paramount purpose should surely be that the subject of the biography is not betrayed, depicted as other, reduced to a cypher for some theory or argument, traduced to fit a convenient available model that suits the writer's own prejudices, or may ensure greater sales via notoriety and controversy. This must be a common temptation: recently biography as a genre has gained immense popularity, and the financial rewards, particularly for publishers, have expanded.

Then there is the material with which biographers work: the evidence about their subjects, the residue, the 'what is left behind' of their lives as lived which underlies their lives as written. For those who are, in research terms, 'safely' dead, say before the turn of last century, the material may be summed up in a word: archives. Even if the material is in the public domain in the form of books, there are always archives attached to publications (publishers' records and files, hand-written drafts, printers' inventories and so on),[6] which may be a rich source of evidence.

Since about the beginning of the twentieth century, however, matters have become more complicated. To the letters, notes, diaries, journals and financial records that are the stuff of archival holdings — whether public or private — must be added far more problematic material such as film, video and speech recordings. These are more difficult to understand because they are selective in some particular, unknowable ways. They have been filmed or recorded by someone with a purpose that may be hard to detect, and perhaps edited with similar consequences. Although date and time of filming/recording, possibly also the details of editing and first screening/playing, can all be established as facts, yet the meaning may, even so, remain obscure.

And the closer we get to the present, the greater the problems become, because much contemporary biography, written about people only recently departed, is dependent on interviews with witnesses who supposedly knew the person and can perhaps testify with authority to some aspect of his or her life. Such interviews are a special instance of what is more generally true, that a lot of what we profess to know is derived from what others tell us. But what they say is not always, for one reason or another, correct, except in the limited but still very interesting sense that it conveys something about the speaker. What the biographer needs to ask is not only *what* is being told, but *why*.

I encountered several instances of this when researching and writing the life of Dan Davin. Condemnation, ridicule or aloof superiority contributed to the tenor of evidence from some Southland relatives and family friends for whom Davin's loss of faith and rejection of his Catholic upbringing constituted apostasy, putting him beyond even sympathy, let alone admiration. They hadn't read his books because they disapproved of him, their minds were already closed to all his labours and they considered his success and recognition in the world to be undeserved.

In a different vein was information from a female contemporary of Davin's future wife, Winnie Gonley, at Otago University. They were both young women some three or four years older than Davin when he arrived there as a freshman in 1931. She wrote me a letter ridiculing him as a tedious adolescent puppy in short trousers. Apart from being somewhat venomous, it was also lively and entertaining, but it added to his biography not so much in its accurate appraisal of him, as in its assistance in clarifying the diverse student life that surrounded him at the very start of his academic career, and the jealousies that abounded within it.

These difficulties can reach close to infinite proportions when it comes to interviewing surviving family members. Infinite because the feelings and sentiments that lie behind the testimony reach far back into complicated matters of psychology: competition for parental attention, alliances with siblings, resentment of hurts inflicted (imaginary and real) bitterness over matters of inheritance, events remembered as instances of neglect or betrayal that touch on unchangeable hurts, slights and presumptions. So melodiously may the family sirens sing that the biographer as interviewer needs to be tied to the mast of scepticism.

Family members are not alone in posing the problem of truth and its telling. What is the biographer to make of the oral testimony of people who have lived their lives in the worlds of politics, diplomacy or security, where being 'economical with the truth' is a professional requirement, a first order one in many cases, and when telling an inconvenient truth may lose you your job, certainly your influence? How would a biographer approach the writing of the life of, say, Stella Rimington, who was director-general of MI5 in the 1990s? Not only would the all-important archives be unavailable, but any oral testimony by or about her, inherently unreliable. This is an extreme case, of course, which would actually make the writing of any reasonably reliable biography of her impossible. But it highlights the more general problem: that much cannot be trusted. And anything that touches on the secret arms of the establishment in whatever country falls into this category. This is because governments trade not only in information, but also on the public's ignorance of it.

Any writer tempted to wade into this treacherous terrain has two main obligations: to remain sceptical of 'official' opinion, especially when not supported by documentary evidence; and, once given some clear assertion of such supposed facts, to pursue their reliability through every possible available avenue. You cannot, for example, just accept the moral duplicity of some figure handed down by an 'authority' because it conforms to your own prejudice, or because it fits neatly into a general design of someone's life that you, or some other interested party, wishes to project. Reliability requires evidence, much of which you may have to admit at the start is completely unknown to you. Justice Robert Megarry's view expressed in the High Court in England is a helpful guide: 'The path of the law is strewn with examples of open and shut cases which, somehow, were not; of unanswerable charges which, in the event, were completely answered; of inexplicable conduct which was fully explained.'[7]

In the lives of famous people friends and acquaintances will often compete for posthumous prominence. I encountered a fair bit of this in Davin's case, made particularly interesting because these people's certainty of their significance in his life was the product of his ability to make them feel as though they were important to him. What was at work was not their stature, but rather his sympathetic friendliness, a humane tolerance that he extended as both a courtesy and a pleasure.

On the other hand, some people of great, even central importance to him, had much less of a presence among the battalions of those willing to talk. Two people in particular declined to be interviewed altogether, for very good and understandable reasons, though in each case the details were impossible to know. A choice of privacy is worthy of respect.

Interviews, once agreed to, raise all sorts of practical dilemmas on which much advice is gladly given: whether to record or not; if not, how to take and keep notes; whether to share a full or partial transcript with the interviewee. Does the respondent have a 'right of reply' to what is written? Must he or she see the draft typescript? And so on. The more important point here is this: the best that can be hoped from oral testimony about the life of another, is help in establishing context. These are the people among whom the subject of the biography spent this or that part of his or her life. They exemplify circumstance. They are evidence of a partial world of experience at some particular time.

Contrary to the modern current of opinion, my belief, rooted in experience, is that the biographer generally does well to remain sceptical of all so-called 'oral history' as a source for anything larger than the specific life of the teller. As it may touch on the particular life of the subject of a biography it should be sanitised with a healthy scepticism lest it infect, like a virus, the whole understanding of another's existence in the world. Truths about experience in a life, the sharp foreground, so to speak, amid and as opposed to the general background, should be sought in the documents.

This view is particularly germane to the problem all biographers face at some stage of their research: how to approach the big things about which we know little or nothing. The most obvious, one is inclined to say universal of these, is childhood. In general, chapter one, 'Childhood', tends to be the shortest in every biography, and for good reason. There is a dearth of dependable evidence. Birth, death and marriage certificates, records of houses occupied, some family reminiscences passed down from one generation to the next and always hard to test for reliability. If you are lucky there may be a few school records, and (in more recent cases) photographs and video — what Sybille Bedford called 'the residue of anecdote and snapshot'.[8] Robert Skidelsky, writing about John Maynard Keynes, refers to the bedrock elements: country, language, class, gender, religion, education. And he is surely right. But the assertion is quickly said, much harder to fill out.

And class presents an added difficulty, not just in the origins of the subject, but in the biographer's search for those origins, because families that are established, well off financially and socially successful, often keep better records, have longer family memories and pass on to their offspring much more about their origins and early life. Without that, the trails go cold within a generation. The contemporary popularity of genealogy, made possible by computer and internet, may add names and dates, but all family trees are shady, as Davin pointed out, and do little to shed light on the individual detail of past family life.[9] There has surely been inheritance, but of what? It is not too far-fetched to assert that if you keep searching back you will only discover that, like all the rest of us, you are descended from Charlemagne.[10]

Bill and Shirley offer interesting contrasting cases of this general problem. Shirley's birth, upbringing and childhood are far better documented than Bill's. Apart from a few small items of family lore, we know next to nothing about him until he seems to spring into life, fully formed, at about the age of 20. His parents left almost no written record and he himself was clearly uninterested in autobiography. Apart from a few scattered remarks about his mother and his upbringing, he is silent. He would have remembered the home front during the First World War. He was 11 when it ended, 12 and 13 during the flu pandemic, yet the biographer would be condemned almost to silence about the impact of these events on his young life, let alone the intimate matters of family experience. For instance, what was his response to the birth of his sister in 1918? We know that he was, in adult life, very fond of her and helped her a great deal. Did this stem from something in her infancy? Was he interim child minder and nappy changer for a two-year-old? Unanswerable questions.

Shirley, on the other hand, coming from a completely different class background, is documented, though to a limited extent, in her own father's hand-written autobiography; in the stories told and retold about her childhood; in the items of remembrance preserved about her mother; and in the stories that she told about herself to her daughter. With this material to hand a biographer ought to be able to paint a clear enough portrait of the young woman who emerged from this background and evolved into the resilient and courageous woman of her full maturity.

The biographer also requires the talent to bring it to the page, to locate Shirley by detail and historical reference in the Wellington and then the Auckland of the immediate post-1918 world and to bring to the surface and examine the life of a family farm in the Waikato of the early 1920s, the isolation, the world of cousins and aunts and uncles to which she was introduced, the complexity of the world for a little girl with no mother and a distant father. The family farm, the physical proximity to stock and their handling, the daily life of toil amid country pleasures: one would need to avoid the danger of imagining these, but instead seek to find hard evidence in the local histories and memoirs of the time and place.[11]

Then, quite suddenly and out of this context, the biographer would have to reverse the flow when Shirley's father remarries and she is called home to a very different household, once again in Wellington, and now separated at the age of seven from her beloved grandmother. Surely that would be worth a question or two, along with some hard sought answers, about the psychology of this particular growing child. And what of its effects on the shape and content of her later life?

These matters are linked to a question all biographers must ask themselves: Am I to write a 'life and times' as opposed to simply a 'life'? In my opinion it would always be best not to separate the two, but when the subject is someone engaged in public affairs, it is surely imperative to locate the figure squarely among the problems of the day. And this is especially so throughout the twentieth century, when many normally politically inactive people were drawn into the public arena by the sheer horror of the events unfolding around them.

The onus is on the biographer to research the history and the background to the period and the place in order to better understand the thoughts, actions, decisions and choices of the subject. The judgements that we make about how to behave, what to say, how to say it are all rooted in the here and now. None of us would want our behaviour to be judged according to the standards of another, very different, future age. Failure to set the detailed historical context risks permitting the reader instinctively to judge past behaviour by the standards and preoccupations of the present, which will almost certainly be a poor fit, if not completely inappropriate. This was always liable to happen to Bill and Shirley.

When Shirley had returned to New Zealand from Oxford — or more accurately, perhaps, from Europe — in 1939, she was still imaginatively engaged with the politics of Europe: the rise of fascism, the defeat of the Republican cause in Spain, German military imperialism. In 1950 her thinking about public affairs was dominated by the swift ascent of what was to become known as McCarthyism — the ruthless pursuit of dissenters, the smear tactics, the deliberate destruction of careers and the fracturing of friendships in a new climate of distrust sparked by propaganda, hatred and intolerance.

Anyone who had not, or did not, toe the line of obedience to orthodox patriotic opinion by expressing 'un-American' beliefs fell victim — the true meaning of victimisation — to the strict orthodoxies of compliance. Shirley had witnessed this, and it reshaped her political commitment towards the issues of civil liberty, in which she became involved soon after she came home. She was active in the creation of a watchdog, the New Zealand Council for Civil Liberties, to represent democratic opinion, to defend victims of discrimination and oppression and to campaign for vigilance on freedom of thought and opinion. It is reasonable to assume that the stimulus for this arose from direct personal experience in New York, which would be a subject of great interest for a biographer. There is a wealth of written material on the rise of McCarthyism, which Shirley would have experienced at first hand.[12]

What seems naïve to us now is the neglect in historical as well as popular New Zealand memory of the transfer to our country of American Cold War McCarthyist belief and conduct. Surveillance and illegal interception of private correspondence by the SIS; the surveillance of lawyers gathered of a Friday evening to have a beer and talk politics while sharing in the purchase of their weekend vegetables, as though they had no right to discussion;[13] the surveillance of university students who dared to republish articles drawn from reputable foreign newspapers, as though they had no right to be interested in world affairs; the wrecking of the public service careers of Paddy Costello, Dick Collins and Doug Lake, as though they had no right to hold opinions that differed from those of security personnel. The propaganda about such things has been at least as successful as the repressive behaviour itself. And this was the New Zealand to which Shirley had returned. It might serve as guidance on the best conduct of biography, which is to understand context and illuminate both action and belief in its light.

This may also serve as a guide to the difference between biography and memoir, which is first and foremost directional. It is hard to see, with biography, how time's arrow can be avoided, since what happens in life unfolds from what came before, and to abandon the logic of the binding ties of history is to rob the subjects of the choices that confronted them. There has been experiment, of course, and not only recently, in structural adaptation away from this logic, but the effect is to diminish the subject in favour of an elevation of the writer, who has chosen to place 'experiment' ahead of subject matter and thereby redirected the focus of the work towards its creator. 'Imaginative interpretation' once again, as offensive to subject and reader alike as, for instance, the invention of conversation in a biography, which implies a familiarity, perhaps even an intimacy with the subject, that is as impossible as it is undeserved.

This cannot be true of the memoir because its author is freely admitting that the work is a personal and particular view of another person, an interpretation of another life written with the writer's own personal emphases. The writer as anecdotalist and raconteur. Furthermore, the memoirist is free to record the impression of another life in whatever order may be preferred. The observations recorded are a summation of what has been learned in the course of a life, a set of often quite fluid and developing adjustments in perception and understanding.

The memoir, in a way, advances backwards, recognising and, where necessary, correcting past error, adjusting understanding in the light of new information and gaining in interpretive understanding through a mellowing of judgement and perception. One might even dare to say insight. But above all else the memoir has the advantage of personal knowledge and experience. It is at only one remove from its subject. Description and analysis do not depend on intervening material, the archives and unreliable interviews. It has the immediacy of an entrée, the sharp quality of privileged knowledge. The biographer, engaged on a completely different enterprise, may sometimes seem impoverished by comparison.

Virginia Woolf's observation that 'Biography is to give a man some kind of shape after his death' is unhelpful, both as guidance and as description or analysis.[14] It suggests imposition by the biographer rather than a quest for the threads of a life that may be quite shapeless, though still imbued with meaning and importance. We tend to look for and to find shape because it satisfies us, it conforms to our aesthetic desires, but as often as not it is absent in a life. What are present, are threads of experience that, once identified, may be seen to stretch out through life, offering definition and some coherence to what otherwise is inchoate, cloudy, ill defined. The biographer's task is to draw those threads out, permitting them, without advertisement, to resonate.

Such faithfulness to uncertainty does not undermine the narrative direction of a life, but it does help to eliminate the idea of plot — a great, evil menace in any account of a life, as though it might be transformed into a detective thriller or a gothic melodrama. It may also help the writer to avoid the pitfall of imagining that any life might turn on some singular incident, which can be transformed into the 'hook' that not only interprets the whole of a life but also sells it as 'The Life' to a public supposedly eager for short-lived entertainment — the Writers and Readers Week, the conference platform, the heady hope for the best-seller lists and the literary prize. The vanity of human wishes.

The injunction to a biographer is straightforward enough: be faithful to the standards of scholarship. For the memoir writer it is perhaps harder. I know deep down that Polonius' advice, 'to thine own self be true', is unhelpful, since I don't know, any more than Hamlet, the self to which I am to respond truthfully. The best I have been able to hope for in this brief memoir of my own is a steady concentration on the lives it has been a privilege to observe, sufficient humility to admit error amid the misgivings to which we are all subject, and the capacity not only to search for what I might know, but the ability to communicate it with the integrity that the subjects deserve.

These hopes, though clearly not the means, might equally be shared, different as their purposes may be, by biographers and memoirists.

Bill and Shirley at Taupō in November 1974, between Bill's arrest in September and his High Court trial the following February. Bill is looking affectionately at the photographer, his daughter, Helen.

The last word

It's incomparably easier to know a lot, say, about the history of art and to have profound Ideas about metaphysics and sociology, than to know personally and intuitively a lot about one's fellows and to have satisfactory relations with one's friends and lovers, one's wife and children. Living's much more difficult than Sanskrit or chemistry or economics.

Philip Quarles in Aldous Huxley's
Point Counter Point

Appendices

These documents, published here as contrasting views, roughly speaking, of the Lion and the Weasel types, all contain errors, which I have left uncorrected as evidence of the ease with which reputation grows from the mischief of misrepresentation.

Appendix A

An Address to Dr. W. B. Sutch from the Staff of the Department of Industries and Commerce on the Occasion of his Retirement as Permanent Head, 31 March 1965.

Over a span of more than forty years William Ball Sutch, retiring Permanent Head of the Department of Industries and Commerce, has been outstanding as a scholar, lecturer, broadcaster, educationalist, economist, planner, author, historian, encourager of the arts, diplomat, international public servant and senior New Zealand public servant.

Dr. Sutch is a distinguished New Zealander, the measure of whose distinction far exceeds the sum of his individual achievements.

His university career led to the award of a university fellowship against world competition; this was followed by his doctorate at Columbia University, New York, in the early nineteen-thirties. Before this Dr. Sutch had already had experience in secondary school teaching, for which he is still widely remembered.

Between 1933 and 1942 he served as an economist and policy adviser to successive Governments. He saw army service and served overseas before an injury brought him back to an essential civilian role in 1943.

He served as economist and policy adviser of UNRRA, South-West Pacific area office. Then it was that he organised the United Nations appeal for children, the forerunner of UNICEF, and also coordinated the work of CORSO with that of the Australian states in supplying goods for war relief. In 1946 and 1947 he served in UNRRA's European office in London as director of a team of economists reporting on the needs of devastated Europe.

From late 1947 to 1951 Dr. Sutch served abroad, as an officer of the Department of External Affairs as the first Secretary-General to the New Zealand Delegation to the United Nations in New York.

He participated conspicuously in the formulation of the United Nations technical assistance programme which he piloted through the Economic and Social Council of the United Nations.

He represented New Zealand on the United Nations Social Commission for three years, at a time when the Commission was active in the establishment of conventions concerning the traffic in persons and narcotics, penal reform and the rights of the child.

In 1948 he was elected Chairman of the United Nations Social Commission and at the request of his fellow members was Chairman for a second year. Also from 1948 to 1951 he was Chairman of the main administrative committees of the UNICEF administration.

From 1951 to 1956 Dr. Sutch served in the Department of Industries and Commerce as Economist, then as Assistant Secretary, and from August 1958 as Secretary of the Department.

Over this time the Department changed from one dealing mainly with price control, trade promotion and import licensing to an organisation vitally concerned with broad economic and development policy. Specifically, the Trade Relations Branch, the Development Division, the Economics Branch, the Industrial Design Section, the Consumers' Institute, the administration of the Trade Promotion Council, the Trade Practices legislation and the beginnings of the Export Guarantee Organisation are among the fruits of his leadership.

He has been similarly responsible for the Department's contribution to the remodelling of the import licensing system, the building of new trade posts abroad and the injecting of a new impetus to the Standards Institute. Never before has the Department moved ahead so rapidly on so many fronts.

Throughout his career, inclination and opportunity have continued to call Dr. Sutch to the service of the aims of broad human betterment and the development of New Zealand as an independent nation.

Within New Zealand he has lectured, written and worked over the whole of his adult life for the under-privileged and neglected. He has been quick to criticise injustices — to the Maori people or to women, for example. Indeed, New Zealand women acknowledge few, if any, more active champions of their cause. As a writer, he has interpreted with insight and deep feeling the social life and history of our country.

Dr. Sutch was foremost among those who from the Coalition Government onwards helped change New Zealand's social, agricultural and financial institutions in the recovery from the great depression of the nineteen-thirties. His hand was prominent in that long list of legislative measures, now accepted as part of our economic and social fabric, which in those days helped lift New Zealand from defenceless depression and set it on the road to economic revival.

Especially during the fourteen years since his return from the broader international field of economic and social affairs, Dr. Sutch has directed his energy into the work of helping build New Zealand as a nation. No one could claim to have done more than he in serving and promoting the cause of industrial development. He was the author of the doctrine of development in depth, now widely accepted in New Zealand, and of the concept of the export of quality manufactures.

Although many will think of Dr. Sutch first as the builder of a new basis, and the guide of a new direction for manufacturing, he is in fact

*an advocate of total balanced development in
all fields. Thus it is, for example, that he has
never accepted the need for conflict between
manufacturing and farming.*

*This total attitude was exemplified in the first
Industrial Development Conference of 1960 and the
Export Development Conference of 1963, models of
administration, as well as of policy formulation,
for which he was personally responsible, and which
have won high praise.*

*The key to his thesis has been people. It begins with
an emphasis on the quality of life, the value of the
human being and the need to discover, nurture
and harness the potentialities of the child so that
he, and society, might be the more enriched. So
it was that he was led again and again to seek in
education the key to the future: few people can have
had his awareness of the role of education in our
economic life.*

*In this he has been his own exemplar: his private
life also has been devoted to adult education, to the
service of the arts and to the improvement of the
New Zealand environment.*

*Those who have been privileged to work with Dr.
Sutch know him as a man of great ability, integrity
and warmth, as unafraid to champion the right as
he is intolerant of the wrong, the insular, and the
short-sighted.*

As his official career ends and we recall the richness of his public service, spontaneous expressions of respect, regard and appreciation for work well beyond the call of duty come from the commercial, manufacturing, professional and private walks of life.

The staff of his Department add to these their own sincere expression of admiration and regard. They salute him for his leadership in so many fields and the executive ability he has always shown; and they thank him for the loyalty, stimulation and practical encouragement that he has so clearly extended to his own staff.

Dr. Sutch goes into private life carrying with him the good wishes of all in the Department and their confidence that he will continue to work towards the building of his country.

Appendix B

Two personal opinions by anonymous witnesses commissioned by the Security Intelligence Service, supposedly in or about 1962, and declassified on 9 May 2008. The last eight lines of the first of these conforms so closely, and with such apparent prescience, to the actual events of 1974–75 that it's hard to believe that the piece has not been, shall we say, 'improved' after the event.

Personal opinion of W. B. Sutch based on information obtained from a close associate in 1962.

WILLIAM BALL SUTCH has displayed one outstanding characteristic throughout his association with source, namely that he is an accomplished actor of many parts., all of which he can play with confidence and ability. The word 'actor' is used intentionally. SUTCH can assume one of a series of roles, each role being assumed in order that he might achieve mastery of every situation. He can be aloof, provocative, egotistical, diplomatic, or assume one of several inter-related guises of mediator, confidant, flatterer or collaborator. In short, SUTCH cannot or will not be categorised professionally or politically; he enjoys being an enigma, probably not intentionally

*because his attitudes of mind appear to be adopted
with one end in view: to gain admiration for every
action undertaken.*

*Aloof, self-opinionated, SUTCH nevertheless
impresses source as fluent in a number of different
subjects. He has a thirst for knowledge, and will
not bear fools easily. SUTCH is contemptuous of
persons regardless of status who cannot follow
and accept his rapid appreciation of a given
problem. That he might fall from grace SUTCH does
contemplate, but his insurance appears to be his
widely publicised accomplishments and influence,
particularly in industrial, commercial and cultural
fields. This prestige and influence SUTCH might
well consider to be his trump card against any
political maneuver that might be set afoot to
unseat him.*

---

*A further opinion of SUTCH by a person who knew
him well, and obtained at about the same time as
the above.*

W. B. Sutch:

*This is a highly intelligent man, with a great
capacity for new and detailed information. His
range of interests is broad, extending from the
technical questions he encounters in his work to all
phases of the arts and social sciences. He is shrewd
and polished, with a well-developed faculty for
dissimulation.*

SUTCH is intrigued with his own considerable erudition, and appears to regret the lack of audiences capable of appreciating fully his versatility and skill. He is is (sic) disdainful of lesser talents, i.e. everyone but W. B. Sutch, and thus is condescending in his attitude to humanity in general.

He is hypocritical in his personal relationships, and sometimes dishonest. Personal loyalty is outside his scope. Wherever possible, he manipulates his associates to his own advantage. Frequently this is easy because SUTCH is intellectually superior to, and mentally quicker than, most of his colleagues.

SUTCH is a cold man, and probably incapable of any truly profound emotion. His greatest gratifications come from nourishment of his ego. Thus, flattery probably is the weapon to which he is most likely to be vulnerable.

Notes

The Lion & the Weasel A memoir of Bill Sutch

I

1 His own doctorate was awarded by what was then, in 1932, the School of Political Science at Columbia University, which incorporated the teaching of economics, possibly indicating the lower academic esteem in which the subject was then held.

2 Plischke was a refugee from Nazi Austria. In the 24 years that he lived in New Zealand (1939–63) he was, with Cedric Firth, Helmut Einhorn and a few others, a leading exponent of architectural modernism. The house he designed for Bill and Shirley has been much written about, discussed and photographed.

3 A big topic for Bill's biographer, Rosslyn Noonan. It was widely believed that Jack Marshall, his minister, could not abide being constantly outflanked by a head of department more knowledgeable and with greater political skills. In his memoirs he denied having had any role in Bill's dismissal — which is what it was, really. The State Services Commission, searching for a peg, discovered that Bill had been a cadet in the public service — then a means of helping promising students through university study — way back in the 1920s, for just long enough that it could be said he had contributed 40 years of service.

4 This delightful book was published for a subscription list that includes the names of almost all the great English estate gardeners of the second half of the eighteenth century.

5 Julia Gatley and Paul Walker, *Vertical Living: The Architectural Centre and the Remaking of Wellington*, Auckland: Auckland University Press, 2014, p. 85.

6 The book was first published in Oslo in 1927. Bill's first edition paperback copy, which he didn't acquire until 1950, was so well read that it had been rebound in quite stylish brown leather. The quotation is from the preface, p. 7.

7 His biographer has told me there is much evidence in Bill's papers

that he knew the 1930s Christchurch artists, writers and musicians Peter Simpson christened 'Bloomsbury South,' and to whom we owe much of the rich evidence for the period from their association with *Tomorrow*. So it is possible that at least some of the first edition Caxton Press poetry and fiction publications that have come down to us were Bill's (I had assumed that they were Shirley's) and that a preoccuption with other tasks and interests excluded them from his table talk later in life.

8   See *Landfall*, No. 81, March 1967, pp. 111–17. Bassett, presumably a man of some perspicacity, remarked at the end of his review: 'I doubt whether there is anyone else in this country with the breadth of vision Sutch possesses. No wonder he casts terror into the ranks of the unregenerate.'

9   J. C. Beaglehole detected similar traits as early as December 1941, calling it 'Awful psychological maladjustment'. Tim Beaglehole, *A Life of J.C. Beaglehole: New Zealand Scholar*, Wellington: Victoria University Press, 2006, p. 311.

10   W. B. Sutch, *Colony or Nation? Economic Crises in New Zealand from the 1860s to the 1960s: Addresses & Papers*, edited by Michael Turnbull, Sydney: Sydney University Press, 1966.

11   Selwyn Lloyd was chancellor of the exchequer in Macmillan's Conservative government from July 1960 to July 1962. National Economic Development Councils were established as part of a strategy to end stop-go economic policies and ensure stable growth by involving government, employers and unions in national agreements. See the *Economist* for coverage of the economics of this government, 1959–63.

12   In addition to all of these works, the list of publications appended to John L. Robson & Jack Shallcrass (eds), *Spirit of an Age: Essays in Honour of W. B. Sutch* (Wellington: A. H. & A. W. Reed 1975) includes many hundreds of other pieces written by Bill: journalism, speeches and contributions to trade journals. Almost without exception, they have only one theme, the understanding and future development of New Zealand.

13   In addition to Bill, three other great administrators headed departments during the Holyoake government: Clarence Beeby at Education, Alister McIntosh at External Affairs and Sam Barnett at Justice. Much of the reputation for intelligent and forward-thinking government that the Holyoake years later attracted was probably largely due to these men, but it is equally probable that their progressive ideas were not much in tune with the National Party politicians whom they must have constantly wrong-footed. Sir John Marshall says as much about Bill in his own memoirs.

14   Ian Milner, *Milner of Waitaki: Portrait of The Man*, Dunedin: Waitaki High School Old Boys' Association, 1983, p.133.

15   John Beaglehole said as much in his private correspondence. See Beaglehole, *A Life of J.C. Beaglehole*, pp. 232, 280, 311.

16   See 'An Address to Dr. W.B. Sutch from the Staff of the Department of Industries and Commerce on the Occasion of his Retirement as Permanent Head 31 March 1965'.

17   Tony Judt with Timothy Snyder, *Thinking the Twentieth Century*, London: William Heineman, 2012, p. 36.

18   There is a good account in Shaun Barnett and Chris Maclean, *Leading the Way: 100 Years of the Tararua Tramping Club*, Wellington: Tararua Tramping Club/Potton & Burton, 2019, pp. 94–99.

19   He dared to repeat it in the greatly expanded 1966 Oxford University Press edition of the same title.

20   There is a full treatment of the truth of this strange matter in Jim Weir's 'Russia Through New Zealand Eyes – to 1944', *New Zealand Slavonic Journal*, 1996, pp. 1–43. In his volume of memoirs, *Eat, Drink and Be Wary* (Wellington: Dunmore Press, 2011), Weir, a long-serving New Zealand diplomat, gives an observant, thoughtful and well-judged appreciation of Bill as he knew him in New York in the late 1940s. Shirley encouraged his article on the 'walk' by giving him access to Bill's letters to his mother, and it knocked on the head an SIS presumption — as so often based on flimsy evidence — that Bill must have been inducted into the NKVD (forerunner of the KGB) while he was on this 'epic' journey. The whole exploit was a foolish brag on Bill's part and probably kicked off his trouble with security services.

II

1   Leonard Woolf, *The Journey Not the Arrival Matters: An Autobiography of the Years 1939 to 1969*, London: Hogarth Press, 1969. Paul Nizan, *Aden Arabie*, translated from the French by Joan Pinkham, New York: Monthly Review Press, 1968, p. 136 (first published in France, 1931).

2   Helen has sought the release of the prosecution file from the trial, but it has been refused.

3   The act was extensively amended as a direct result of Bill's trial. A US Embassy official, reporting on 'cocktail circuit gossip' about Bill's arrest in a telegram to Washington of September 1974, wrote: 'Under U.S. Law, [the] evidence might seem insufficient [as] the Official Secrets Act places burden of proof on accused to show he has not been in communication with a foreign agent.' Telegram from Killgore at American Embassy,

Wellington to State Department, R030500Z, 1 October 1974, declassified 30 June 2005. (Other informative telegrams were declassified at the same time and are available on the State Department website. Still others remain secret.) American law required evidence that information had changed hands. This explains, I think, the SIS determination to maintain they knew that something written had been passed. Even though it wasn't strictly necessary for the prosecution to proceed, it would have impressed their American counterparts and colleagues. They just couldn't produce any evidence of it.

4   The paranoia of both the American and the Russian authorities through the 1950s, 1960s and 1970s is no doubt hard to understand for those who never experienced its effects, or who have been born since, but it was real and needs to be kept in mind.

5   Just a few hours after Bill's acquittal, Helen and I witnessed the arrival at the Brooklyn house of a young woman we both knew well. After declining to stay for what was turning into an impromptu celebration, she quickly congratulated him with a kiss that spoke of a great deal more than a well-wisher's amity, then left. That moment, and the insight it brought, have never left me.

III

1   Qualities they demonstrated yet again when they turned up to photograph mourners at Bill's funeral. What were they thinking?

2   This is the only time, to my knowledge, that the SIS has ever admitted to its incompetence over the affair, but it appears to do so only because of its convenience to their general argument. The suggestion was aired by a later SIS head, who talked frankly, and apparently on the record, to a biographer. It is hard not to think that he was himself in breach of the confidentiality laws governing SIS personnel during both their employment and their retirement, and is a good example of the special dispensation they allot to themselves when they believe they are entitled to do so.

3   Kirk's secretary had a malicious say about the matter in her diary. Margaret Hayward, *Diary of the Kirk Years*, Wellington: Reed, 1981.

4   Helen Clark behaved with scrupulous decency. In 2007 Helen (my wife) was invited to meet the then head of the SIS to be informed of and to discuss the decision to release the file. She requested that the release be delayed until after Shirley, by this time very much reduced, had died. This was agreed to and the file was not released until the winter of 2008, when it came to Helen, out of

courtesy, a month before it was made public. The SIS head made it clear that they held no other material about her father.

5   United Press International reported on 21 September 2005: 'KGB's operation in India was its largest in the world and the Soviet agency had to open a new department to handle the material coming from India.' With such a colossal waste of money and administrative focus is it surprising that the Soviet regime collapsed?

6   See Beverley Randell and Roger Steele (eds), *Hugh Price, Publisher*, Wellington: Steele Roberts, 2012, p. 101.

7   See his *Final Approaches: A Memoir*, Auckland: Auckland University Press, 2006, p. 222. The two positions, Hensley's and Whim Wham's, are indicative of the thesis that was coming into focus for me, side by side in popular discourse.

8   Permission to quote from 'How Guilty is Sin?' by Whim Wham courtesy of the copyright owner Tim Curnow, Sydney.

9   Christopher Andrew and Vasili Mitrokhin, *The Mitrokhin Archive: The KGB in Europe and the West*, London: Penguin Books, 2000, and *The Mitrokhin Archive II: The Rest of the World*, 2005. Publications from the archive also include *The KGB Lexicon: The Soviet Intelligence Officer's Handbook*, London: Frank Cass & Co. Ltd, 2002. There is a straight-faced narrative account of how Mitrokhin's defection was handled by the British in the Parliamentary Intelligence and Security Committee's *Mitrokhin Inquiry Report*, June 2000, Cmnd 4764.

10   *Mitrokhin Inquiry Report*, paras 26–41.

11   Peter Padfield, *Hess, Hitler & Churchill: The Real Turning Point of the Second World War – A Secret History*, London: Icon Books, 2013, p. 19. The quotation is from Richard J. Aldrich, *The Hidden Hand: Britain, America, and Cold War Secret Intelligence*, London: John Murray, 2001.

12   Dan van der Vat, Pik Botha Obituary, *Guardian*, 12 October 2018.

13   Tony Judt, 'A Story Still to be Told', review of *The Cold War: A New History* by John Lewis Gaddis (New York: Penguin, 2006) *New York Review of Books*, 23 March 2006.

14   There is a wealth of material on this. See Amy Knight, 'Leonard?', *Times Literary Supplement*, 26 June 2009, which contains guidance on how the newly opened (and then closed again) files of the Russian secret service agencies should be handled by Western researchers. She is particularly good on how the Soviet agents in foreign countries in the early Cold War years, terrified of their Moscow bosses, padded reports with material about contacts and made untrue and fanciful claims about recruiting spies. In short, much of what passes for

intelligence gathering and proof of spying by named Western contacts in the Soviet files is quite possibly untrue, and most definitely so in many cases.

15   Herbert Romerstein, 'A Valuable New Book on the KGB', review of John Earl Haynes, Harvey Klehr and Alexander Vassiliev, *Spies: The Rise and Fall of the KGB in America* (New Haven: Yale University Press, 2009) Right Side News. The Right News for Americans, rightsidenews.com, 13 May 2009. Romerstein is the co-author, with Eric Breindel, of *The Venona Secrets: Exposing Soviet Espionage and America's Traitors* (Washington: Simon & Schuster, 2000), and was for 18 years a professional staff member of the US Congress House Committee on Un-American Activities.

16   John Marshall, *Memoirs, Volume Two 1960–1988*, Auckland: Collins, 1989, pp. 141–9.

17   The two assessments (Appendix B) are said to date from 1962, close to the time of the National Party's return to power. They can be read as responding to the question of whether Bill could be removed from office by an incoming government.

18   You have to be careful with this sort of thing, though. Claud Cockburn, to whom he was said to have leaked the news, was the greatest exponent of what we now call fake news. He published lots of it in his 1930s news sheet, *The Week*, and confessed how he made things up in his entertaining, but possibly unreliable, *I Claud . . . An Autobiography*, London: Penguin, revised edition, 1965. There is more evidence of it in Patricia Cockburn, *The Years of the Week*, London: Macmillan, 1968; Penguin, 1971. When I retrieve my own copies of these wonderful books from the shelves I see that Helen and I first read them in Wellington in 1971, just as I was getting to know Bill for the first time.

19   'Sometimes it is years before we can see who are the heroes in an affair and who are the victims. Martyrs don't reckon with the results of their actions. How can they when their mind is only on how to endure pain?', Hilary Mantel, *The Mirror and the Light*, London: Fourth Estate, 2020, p. 432.

If only, if only . . . A memoir of Shirley Smith

I

1   Vintage, 2003. Principally James Bertram, Charles Brasch, Geoffrey Cox, Dan Davin and Ian Milner, with sideline appearances by Paddy Costello, Norman Davies and John Mulgan.

II

1   My favourite is Styra Avins (ed.), *Johannes Brahms: Life and Letters*, Oxford: Oxford University Press, 1997. By way of contrast, see Caroline Moorehead's *A Bold and Dangerous Family: One Family's Fight Against Italian Fascism*, Auckland: Penguin, 2018. The book is based on her reading of many thousands of private letters, yet she barely quotes from any of them.

2   Aldous Huxley writing in 1950 to his friend Edwin Hubble, the astronomer, about his work on Maine de Biran, quoted in Sybille Bedford, *Aldous Huxley: A Biography, Volume II*, London: Collins/Chatto & Windus, 1974, p. 110.

3   Private correspondence, Sir Geoffrey Cox to Keith Ovenden, 22 March 1996. Permission to quote courtesy of the estate of Sir Geoffrey Cox.

III

1   There is a good account of these obstacles in Helen Wilson's *My First Eighty Years* (Hamilton: Paul's Book Arcade, 1951), p. 155, where she describes a bicycle trip in January 1903.

2   As well as the very successful autobiography, *My First Eighty Years*, she wrote an entertaining novel, *Moonshine* (1942), and the semi-fictional *Land of My Children* (1955).

3   From No. 5 of *Twenty Sonnets of W. M. Smith* by Christopher Caudwell (1907–1937), the nom de plume of English poet, novelist, critic Christopher St John Sprigg. A member of the Communist Party of Britain, he was killed in the Spanish Civil War.

4   Bungay Greig was the name of the law firm. Ian Greig was the brains. A quiet, thoughtful man with a very original mind, he was not made for the public arena, though he was, for many years, greatly valued and admired as president of the Port Nicholson Yacht Club. A steady man in a storm.

5   This was not surprising. One of the great adversarial lawyers of his time, and a good friend to Shirley throughout her legal career. See Gary Turkington, 'William Vernon Gazley 1921–2011', *Council Brief*, April 2011.

6   Not immensely valuable, however. I have seen similar genuine Han equestrian figures in an antique shop in Sydney (though this was a few years ago) selling for $5000. Bill had bought this one in New York in the late 1940s, when many Chinese immigrants, fleeing the victory of Mao's Communist Party in 1948, were eager to sell works that they had brought with them.

7   George Hamish Ormond Wilson (1907–1988), politician,

conservationist, historian. There is a fine entry by Janet Paul in *Te Ara*: 'Wilson, George Hamish Ormond', Dictionary of New Zealand Biography, first published in 2000. Te Ara – the Encyclopedia of New Zealand, https://teara.govt.nz/en/biographies/5w37/wilson-george-hamish-ormond

Between memoir & biography A note on lives lived in words

1   First published in the *New York Herald Tribune*, 30 October 1927; republished in *Virginia Woolf, Collected Essays*, Volume Four, London: Hogarth Press, 1967, pp. 229–35. Much of the essay is an attack on nineteenth-century biography and might be read as a settling of scores of some sort with her father who was, after all, founder and first editor of the *Dictionary of National Biography*. And why did Leonard Woolf, her widower, who edited these essays towards the close of his own life, insert this piece and a companion essay, right at the very end of the final volume? Was he trying to say something, just inaudible, out of our reach?

2   In these reflections I have profited greatly from a few exemplary works: Ulick O'Connor, *Biographers and the Art of Biography*, Dublin: Wolfhound Press, 1991; Bruce Redford, *Designing the Life of Johnson, the Lyell Lectures, 2001–2*, Oxford University Press, 2002; Robert Zaretsky and John T. Scott, *The Philosophers' Quarrel: Rousseau, Hume, and the Limits of Human Understanding*, New Haven: Yale University Press, 2009.

3   An ugly neologism implying facility in what is extremely difficult. Carlyle employed it, disparagingly, when reviewing Lockhart's *Walter Scott*. It has slipped into the common vernacular, however, only in the twenty-first century largely, perhaps, to embrace the rapidly expanding field of memoir, in particular that of millennials rich in their struggles with oppression, victimhood, drug dependence, self-harm and sexual indiscretion. We may, in due course, look forward to the genre of death-writing though, it is to be hoped, rather later in these fledgling literary careers.

4   Philip Roth, quoted by Nathaniel Rich in *New York Review of Books*, 28 June 2018, p. 14.

5   Johnson, Boswell, Strachey, Woolf, Holroyd, Holmes, Moorehead – biographers' names make a canon by repetition, but their works are incomparable. Diversity is the key. People cannot be made to fit a theory. Each writer's approach to the intellectual matter and the lived experience of the subjects

is what distinguishes one biographer from another. Readers must judge the level of application, and in the service of what objective, in each case. Across the broad field of contemporary biography, many fail the test.

6   See D. F. McKenzie, *Making Meaning: 'Printers of the Mind' and Other Essays*, Amherst: University of Massachusetts Press, 2002; and John Thomson, ed., *Books and Bibliography: Essays in Commemoration of Don McKenzie*, Wellington: Victoria University Press, 2002.

7   Louis Blom Cooper, 'Sir Robert Megarry', obituary, *Guardian*, 19 October 2006.

8   In *Aldous Huxley: A Biography*, Vol.1, 1894–1939, p. 2.

9   Arguments further elaborated by Kate Clanchy in her review: 'Common People: The History of an English Family', *Guardian*, 18 October 2014.

10 This, and much else besides, is tellingly illuminated in Michael Thompson, *Rubbish Theory*, Oxford: Oxford University Press, 1979.

11 A good place to start would be Helen Wilson's *My First Eighty Years*, Hamilton: Paul's Book Arcade, 1952. Her granddaughter, Shirley's beloved sister-in-law Helen Smith, had grown up on the farm her grandmother had helped to break in after the First World War. The connection to her own childhood experiences in the Waikato countryside at exactly this time strengthened Shirley's bond with Helen.

12 Shirley attempted to write about this for our older son when he was given a school essay on the subject, but her memory had by then begun to weaken and the attempt failed.

13 The vegetable club. At least one SIS informant infiltrated it and collected accounts of the opinions expressed. Its members were apparently held in suspicion and kept under surveillance for years. Some descendants of the original members, out of piety and admiration for their forebears and some contempt for what was done to them, have reconstituted the club, which meets occasionally in Wellington.

14 The curse of the quotation for the memoirist. He knows that Virginia Woolf wrote these words, but is unable to track down where exactly. He would be glad to hear from anyone who can find the source which he, profligate, has misplaced.

Acknowledgements

I am grateful to a small number of friends who read and commented on an early draft of this memoir; to the publisher, production manager and editor at Massey University Press for their creative and unselfish diligence and their confidence in and patience with a difficult manuscript and its author; to the estate of John Clarke for permission to quote from an email to the author of 31 Januray 2008; and to the principal of St Hugh's College, Oxford, the Rt Hon. Dame Elish Angiolini, DBE, QC, FRSE, for her generous and thoughtful help in supplying the photographs of the college and its grounds.

MASSEY UNIVERSITY PRESS

First published in 2020 by Massey University Press
Reprinted 2020
Private Bag 102904, North Shore Mail Centre
Auckland 0745, New Zealand
www.masseypress.ac.nz

Design by Gideon Keith
Cover photograph by Helen Sutch, November 1974

A catalogue record for this book is available from the National Library
of New Zealand

Printed and bound in China by Everbest Printing Investment Limited

ISBN: 978-0-9951318-3-5
eISBN: 978-0-9951378-8-2

ARTS COUNCIL OF NEW ZEALAND TOI AOTEAROA
The assistance of Creative New Zealand is
gratefully acknowledged by the publisher